LINCOLN CHRISTIAN COLLEGE

W9-CBV-461

Redeeming Eve

Redeeming Eve

Finding Hope beyond the Struggles of Life

Heather P. Webb

Baker Books
A Division of Baker Book House Co
Grand Rapids, Michigan 49516

© 2002 by Heather P. Webb

Published by Baker Books
a division of Baker Book House Company
P.O. Box 6287, Grand Rapids, MI 49516-6287

Printed in the United States of America

All rights reserved. No part of this publication may be reproduced, stored in a retrieval system, or transmitted in any form or by any means—for example, electronic, photocopy, recording—without the prior written permission of the publisher. The only exception is brief quotations in printed reviews.

Library of Congress Cataloging-in-Publication Data is on file at the Library of Congress, Washington, D.C.

ISBN 0-8010-1245-7

Unless otherwise noted, Scripture is taken from the HOLY BIBLE, NEW INTERNATIONAL VERSION®. NIV®. Copyright © 1973, 1978, 1984 by International Bible Society. Used by permission of Zondervan. All rights reserved.

Scripture marked MESSAGE is taken from THE MESSAGE. Copyright © by Eugene H. Peterson 1993, 1994, 1995. Used by permission of NavPress Publishing Group.

"You're Aging Well" written by Dar Williams © 1993 BURNING FIELD MUSIC (ASCAP)/Administered by Bug. All rights reserved. Used by permission.

"She's Just Dancing" by David Patrick Wilcox copyright © 1980 by Irving Music, Inc., on behalf of itself and Midnight Ocean Bonfire Music (BMI). All rights reserved. Used by permission.

For current information about all releases from Baker Book House, visit our web site:

http://www.bakerbooks.com

For Kirk
A tender man, strong and steadfast

1350

113893

Contents

Acknowledgments

God seems to enjoy surprising us. With most of my writing, teaching, and counseling endeavors, words seem to arise from a place of struggle and hope, joy and sorrow, in my own life. *Redeeming Eve* is no exception. There is a certain accountability in having to live the words one is writing. I have not been immune to the message but have felt called to live it with integrity. This book reflects my own journey. I invite you to journey with me into your own story. It is my hope that you will be richer for it.

Countless voices from the past have helped shape my vision. Each book I have read, every story I have heard, each person I have encountered has added fragments of meaning to the stories I tell.

I wish to thank my former teacher and current colleague Dan Allender whose fingerprints are found throughout this book. My other teachers, though not mentioned by name, include the courageous women and men who have invited me on their journeys as clients, directees, and students. This book flowed out of watching many others live well.

This book's birth was realized through the loving encouragement of friends and family who assisted in the arduous process of labor and delivery. They have been my support. Among them, my husband, Kirk Webb; Christie Lynk; and Betsy and Geoff Parkinson provided the initial editing. Friends and family are witnesses to me of God's transformative love and unending grace.

My thanks extend to Baker Book House for Bob Hosack's passionate overseeing of the project and for the editorial department's wisdom that clarified and strengthened my words.

Finally, I wish to thank my students at Mars Hill Graduate School who helped choose the name for the book and who encouraged me to write my words for others to hear.

Prologue

What does it mean to be a woman who is in the process of healing and who, ultimately, has healing to offer?

What is broken?

What might I hear if I turned my ear inward to hear my heart speak?

These are the unspoken words of the women who sit across from me.

As a counselor, I have the rare privilege of being with people in some of their deepest questions and struggles with God and themselves. I have listened to their stories and been witness to the mysterious process of change.

A tired-looking, middle-aged woman settled into the seat across from me with a sigh. She began to explain in a rapid, staccato manner about her concerns and worries for her children. She ended her monologue with these words: "So you see my problem; I am here hoping you can help me get my son on the right track. He needs to go back to high school and get his degree." Mary looked at me beseechingly, but also with the kind of intensity that said, "I mean business." I knew that she wanted to hear the five short steps to wiring our children to fit our goals for their lives. I knew I had no such tool in my toolbox. Instead, I looked at her and asked, "Is there anything you want personally from counseling that might be of help to you in this situation?" Her look suggested, "Haven't you heard a word I said?" We stared at each other for a few moments, until she broke the silence with, "I guess I am just so tired of carrying this weight around with me." That was an honest admission.

It would take several more months of working together before Mary started talking about herself and her condition instead of the difficult people in her life she was trying to straighten out. Mary had spent many years believing that her worth came only from being able to help someone. She did not believe that there was anything within her own self to be enjoyed.

On another occasion, a vivacious, chipper coed sat across from me. She was all smiles and giggles until she reached the part of her story that was central to her recent problems. Laura got quiet and then glanced up at me nervously. "All my friends are applying to graduate school or interviewing with businesses," she said. "I can't even imagine filling out a job application. People keep asking me what I am going to do with the rest of my life, but I try to blow off the question and change the subject. I have no idea what I am supposed to be when I grow up." Over the next month, it became evident there was more on her mind than just vocation.

Later, speaking in a pained and mature tone, Laura confided that she wasn't sure she wanted to get married, or even could get married, given the fact that she had been brutalized on a date a year ago. The event had occurred in the fall, shortly before Christmas. When she went home at break, her family and friends noticed a change in her, but she would not tell them what had happened. She felt responsible for what happened to her because she had been drinking, which, besides being illegal, was considered a taboo by her family and church. In addition, she felt she had committed what she called the "ultimate sin" of engaging in premarital sex. "I didn't even want it. I certainly didn't enjoy it. But there was no excuse. It's my fault. If only I hadn't had those drinks, that guy wouldn't have been able to take advantage of me and maybe then I could tell my family. But I'm afraid they'll say I was bad, so I've kept this all a secret."

Like Laura, many women are trapped in scripts of regret, wishing desperately to change an inflexible past. They are haunted by the desire to be responsible so they can assure themselves, "This will never happen to me again." It is a way of saying, "If I can take responsibility, I can reassert my control over my life and I can stay safe." But can we stay safe? Is safety the kind of life God intends for us, or is the call for women of faith to something much deeper and broader than safety at all costs?

Mary's and Laura's stories are not unique. They epitomize many stories of the women (and even some of the men) who have sat across from me and wondered about their lives, their purposes, their futures, and their dreams. Certain questions come up frequently: "Will a man ever find me attractive, given my story? How do I find a future when I am living in a broken present? How do I get back to my own story when everyone else's has seemed so important for so long?" With Mary and Laura, as with the other women in this book, names and circumstances have been modified to protect confidentiality. The stories you read are an amalgam of different people's lives and experiences.

13

Many women come to me because they want to recover lost dreams. They feel they are without a future because they have lost sight of the past. They seek to be restored to a sense of God's call and of God's desire for relationship with them. They want to be women of healing but have lost their way. They come to me asking if there is a way back, a path that will lead them to remember who they are in God—to the heart of God.

Our creation story begins in a Garden with the first two inhabitants enjoying a unique relationship of openness and intimacy with their Creator. Soon into the plot, their idyllic life is shattered. Eve had to live the rest of her days knowing that more of all that is good, including God's direct presence, was available in a Garden from which she and Adam had been expelled. That regret and desire for a past of belonging and innocence parallels the experience of many women I know. They can relate to Eve. Something has been lost that cannot be regained. What is required to redeem our losses in a world of toil and suffering? I have often wondered about Eve's story. The "mother of all living" had to bear the death of one of her sons at the hands of his brother. Did Eve ever taste something of healing or redemption in her life outside the Garden? Like Eve, many women seek healing from their past to find meaning for their present. Women of healing are women who love the power redemption has to transform something broken into something beautiful and of great value in God's hands.

There are times in our lives when we feel hungry for something more. Whether it is due to the changes in our lives, our search for a career or a soulmate, midlife, empty nest, or loss of a loved one, we seek spiritual food to ease our hunger pains. We are not content to pretend about our lives anymore; rather, we set about to rekindle our soul's hearth. Renewed intimacy with God, deepened love, laughter with others, and a richer contentment with ourselves are trademarks of a woman of healing.

What is your heart telling you about how you might live out your call as a Christian more authentically? In order to become a person of healing (receiving it and having it to give), you must listen to your life. Your stories, the way you live today, and the dreams you are willing to hold for the future provide a window into God's work in you. These factors invite you to make new choices, to become transformed, and to receive more of what God and others may have for you. In the busyness of life, it takes a determined effort to look within and listen for God's still small voice. What you find there may surprise you.

I

Story, Soul, and Substance

Counseling has taught me, again and again, the truth that our stories reveal our soul's substance or character. How we live, the choices we make, and the events that happen to us shape and mold who we are becoming.

What I call our substance is the weight of who we are, being aware of our God-given value. Whether we feel substantial as women is connected to believing we have words to speak that will matter to others. We have a voice worth hearing. Unfortunately, many women do not believe in the force and weight of their own words; they have felt silenced or stifled.

As well, we are women of healing as we come to appreciate God's gift of a soul. We find an increasing sense of purpose and meaning in God's call, not only as we listen to the stories our lives are telling but also as we offer what God has given to us for the sake of others.

The secular world describes substance as self-esteem, self-awareness, or even self-actualization. Perhaps a word that is more comfortable for people of faith is self-worth. If you believe that you are created by a loving God who fashioned you in God's own image, then you must have worth. No matter who you are. Self-worth is a way of saying your life matters. Your existence is significant on a larger plane than what you see. There is some reason that you have been asked to show up on earth today, and there is some part for you to play. Your part has eternal consequences.

Every so often, we get glimpses of the transcendent story, but only enough to sustain us. We don't get the full story yet. This can be frustrating or it can be freeing. It can free us when we realize that our hope and desire for more is itself a sign that there *is* more, perhaps not more that we will see or know next week, month, or year, but there is something beyond the seen and the tangible.

This drama invites us to look more deeply at who we are and what we have to contribute. Actors spend years training to access deeper parts of themselves to be credible and powerful when playing different roles: They take a journey within to offer something outside themselves to others. Each of us is invited to do likewise.

How Our Stories Shape Us

When we take a journey within, we discover many different facets of who we are. We will find aspects that we wish weren't there. We will recognize that there are stories we have long buried in an effort to escape them. But we will also discover aspects of who we are that are lovely, good, pure, noble, even beautiful. These have often been buried as well.

Our stories add to the substance of who we are and give us meaning. After all, it is difficult to disappear when you remember all the stories of your past and present. They reconnect us to the characters of our past (and present), as well as to our Creator. The writers of the Old Testament heed the call to remember who God is, who his people are, and how God has intervened on their behalf. The feasts and sacrifices were centered around recalling stories of God's redemptive work for his people. The exodus was a crucial story calling all Jews to remember God's provision, deliverance, and protection. The sacrifices reminded Israel of her impurities and need for purification before a holy and just God. Prophets were forever reminding Israel of her first love, nagging them to recall their forgotten story of being people set apart for a purpose. Those stories and ours are avenues back to God's invitation to a relationship with him that we are called to participate in and enjoy.

Definition of a Soul

What is a soul? A precise definition has evaded theologians and moral philosophers over the centuries. How do we define something so intangible, so ephemeral? A soul is that part of us that connects with God because it is the place God's unique image is made known. Perhaps it is easiest to define it in story. Picture a scene in the Garden, found in a story in Genesis. We come upon the first man and woman. We are told that after God took clay to form man's body, there was something still needed. An element of construction, which had not been added, withheld life from this inanimate form. That missing piece was the breath of God that, when God breathed into Adam's nostrils, made him the first living human being. So our souls might be defined as the breath of God. They are that element of God in each of us. A soul is something we are made with, but it is not made once and then finished. Our future choices and decisions play a part in shaping it. How have you shaped your soul? Have you been good to that part of you that reflects God's image and calls us to more than our earthly, material existence?

Women of Substance

Rachel is a single woman who gets home late every night from work. As she tries to unwind, she finds stress from the day running through her head. Questions torment her: *Should I go out or stay in? Will any of my friends call? How long should I wait before giving up?* Rachel wonders where she is supposed to be in life. This is not what she expected her life would be when she was thirty-six. Her life has not worked out as planned. She has forgotten how to listen to her heart and allow it to be a place for hope, rest, purpose, and worship.

April is a mother of young children. She takes care of everyone else—cleaning, feeding, bathing, scheduling, carpooling. She responds to her spouse but finds it difficult to have space for him in her overcrowded, demanding life. There is little time to rest, think, or breathe. April remembers days when she had time for dreaming, when there was space for herself, friends, and God. Now when she has free time, she is so used to being busy and caring for others that the time gets filled with busyness as a distraction, maybe even an addiction. She is no longer intentional about nurturing something within her.

We all search for meaning in the mundane, sense in the chaos, rest from unending demands. We need to keep the stories of Rachel and April in mind. We need to remember that our stories, souls, and substance are significant and require time, effort, and patience.

Our stories shape us. Our souls define our connection to our Maker. These two play important parts in figuring out what it means to be a woman of substance. Although it may take a few minutes to remember, I would venture a guess that each woman can recall a time in her life when she knew she had been powerful. I don't mean by this term a false sense of "my manipulation worked" or "I really showed him." I am describing that sense of release when something flows out of us that touches someone else: providing words of comfort or constructive feedback, stating an opinion that shed light on a difficult situation, and calling for justice in an unjust situation are examples of moments that you knew your words mattered and you needed to be present for that person or situation. You were fully there, and you played a part in the life of another that had consequences beyond the moment and perhaps even beyond the relationships that were present.

We feel substantial when we are living, speaking, and loving out of a place that feels strong and good. When we act out of this strength, we are not worried about defending our rights at all times. Rather, acting out of substance and strength means that we are willing to own our weakness and offer forgiveness to those who have wronged us and, at times, to ourselves. It is living out of a sense of aliveness because we realize we are worth being a self. We know that our existence must be for some higher purpose than may be evident in our present circumstances.

A healing woman has tasted moments of allowing her substance to bless others, knowing as she does that she is being faithful to God's call in her life. She regularly remembers these moments because they testify to the woman she is becoming in God.

Story, soul, and substance are the backdrop to the places we will travel together in this book. They open the door to our exploration of the issues of how we live in a broken state and what it means to move toward holy enjoyment.

Our story, and the stories of those around us, are impacted by the choices we make, which, in turn, often reflect our sense of self-worth. At times we diminish ourselves and end up hiding the good in us. Perhaps the substance of who we are has all but disappeared to those closest to us. This can grieve them, especially when they have gotten a taste of the soul and substance we offer, and they know what they are missing. This can carry a heavy cost for family members and loved ones. The impact of our choices, story, and self-worth extends beyond those close to us and includes all whom our lives touch.

Felicity—One Woman's Story

She spoke eloquently of her days in the inner city. Felicity had resisted the temptations of her friends in the 'hood. She had tried to find solace from the violence of gunshots at night, her grief over her brother's death, and the absence of a father whom she had never known. The violent stories she told were quite a contrast to her calm, professional demeanor. Her chosen vocation surprised me. I eagerly awaited the story.

Felicity had grown up aware that her experience as a minority meant that she received fewer privileges, weaker protection from the law, and was subject to a prejudiced justice system. She decided to become a public defender to offer much-needed legal aid to the people with whom she had grown up. Because retaining her services came at a nominal fee, nonminority clients sought her out. It was then that Felicity realized the state of her heart toward nonminority persons. Felicity told me, "I realized I had become prejudiced in the ways that I did not want others to treat me. It was a frightening day when I became aware that I had become what I hated."

After much soul searching, Felicity decided to open her practice to everyone and offered to help those whom she had experienced as "enemies" of her people. As she saw their fears, neediness, and dreams, her heart became tender toward them. She decided that opening her practice wasn't enough, that she needed to move from law to love, so she offered to facilitate an interfaith, interracial dialogue in her community. She knew that change needed to begin with each individual heart in order to bring about change on a systematic level. Her ministry of reconciliation brought her peace and hope.

It was in this context that we began the journey through stories of the past that Felicity had tried to forget and erase. She had closed her heart to the pain of remembering. A lost brother, an unknown father—these were heavy losses to finally grieve and put to rest. She was now strong enough to face them and let them go.

What motivates someone like Felicity to become an ambassador of reconciliation? Inspired by the words of 2 Corinthians 5:13–21 about Christ giving us the ministry of reconciliation, she decided not to hold people's sin against them. She worked to remove hostility in her own heart and then to see people with heavenly vision as new creations. Her courage came because she was compelled by Christ's love. When her soul was warmed by faith, and she rediscovered and appreciated her story, her substance was freed. Felicity became a powerful change agent for her community and her God.

Biblical Witness

Jesus as Master Storyteller

Jesus spoke in story. Stories were his method for teaching his followers and adversaries about his identity, mission, and kingdom. He made it clear that not all would have "eyes to see and ears to hear." Many times his disciples asked—we can imagine with some degree of consternation—"Now what did that mean? Can you tell it to me straight, Master?" Why was Jesus a storyteller?

Jesus knew that stories have a way of getting under our skin and of explaining the mysterious. They can put substance to an emotion, concept, or reality in a way that outweighs a well-crafted apologetic. He established the basis for a new theology out of stories about common aspects of life: grain, mountains, lilies, widows, and fishermen. He spoke so that all who heard could connect, on some level, with the wisdom the stories contained. His stories provoke his readers to action and to faith. This was all part of his plan to reconcile the world to God.

Through Christ, you have the privilege of inviting others to reconcile their hearts to God and others. This is a high calling—to be both a priest and a prophet. Someone's heart may need softening in places of hardness, or they may need ears to hear in places of deafness, sight in places of blindness. Will you offer the varied gifts of words and presence that Jesus perfectly offered each soul he encountered? What needs to be reconciled in you before that is possible: your past, future, parents, church, friends? And ultimately through, in, and despite all the rest, your Maker?

Do you have a heart for the people in Scripture for whom God has deep compassion? God often calls our attention to the orphans, aliens, widows, poor, sick, disabled, and outsiders. Who are our modern Gentiles or lepers? Jesus healed many and provides us with an example of offering specific gifts to others. He knew perfectly what each person he encountered needed: a firm call, a gentle rebuke, a gracious hand of forgiveness, or a knowing conversation.

Study Questions

What does it mean for me personally to remember my story, my life history? What emotions do I feel as I consider doing so?

The elements from the past I wish to forget are . . .

Those aspects of my story I love to remember include . . .

What are the moments I have felt substantive, when I knew I had something God wanted me to offer to someone else? (Spend some time coming up with a list of several memories.)

What is it like to imagine telling someone else about these experiences?

Have I ever had the opportunity to tell someone my story? What prevents me from sharing more with my friends and family now?

2

Encountering Men

Men Are from Mars, Women Are from Venus.[1] This popular book title speaks to the peculiarities of how men and women relate to each other. A fitting slogan for those embarking on relationships with the opposite sex would be the words inscribed over the haunted house ride at the local amusement park: "Beware, exercise caution, enter at your own risk." Encountering the other, who is mysterious and different, is not easy. It can be unsettling, disruptive, and confusing. My husband tells me, "One day you are fine with something. The next you are angry. I don't know which is really true." Clearly, my womanly ways are a mystery to him, as are his manly ways to me.

It is clear that women are a mystery to men, but it is also fair to say that women are a mystery to themselves. If this is not obvious, note how many times women will say things to discredit or dismiss themselves or their opinions. "This dress? I made it myself, but I didn't do a very good job." Many women are self-deprecating to avoid what being known in relationship might require. Part of this not wanting to be seen is learned behavior. We have listened to and taken notes subconsciously of what others tell us we should be; at times, these others include mothers, fathers, peers, teachers, bosses, and our cultural heritage. They may have conveyed a message such as: "You need to sacrifice your career or dreams for what others expect of you." We have minded the rules and learned to play even if no one sat us down and talked it through with us.

Attitudes—Ours and Others'

"The rules" predate all of our earthly existence and are different from culture to culture and even family to family. One of the realities of being female is that, in most cultures throughout recorded history, we have been the "lesser" sex. Men wrote the books, recorded the history, studied in school, and defined movements by their might. They ruled the power structures of most cultures and set a place for women. At times, that place honored what women contributed, but most often, it has confined and restricted women.

It does not require extensive research to defend the argument that women have long been shut out of positions of leadership, power, and authority, and therefore have not had their voices heard. That has been true in terms of positions of political, corporate, academic, and ecclesial authority. Have you heard of any male-dominated denominational sessions that invited the women of the church to come and share their perspective on what is lacking in worship? Or how well or poorly the church is ministering to those in need? I regret I have not heard of any having done so. I do hold out hope that change is possible in this arena.

Although attitudes about women have changed in the past century in our North American culture, there are still vestiges of discrimination and disdain. A pejorative word for a field in which women have entered or are dominant is the "feminization" of that profession. A job that is considered "woman's work" garners little respect and is perceived as less powerful than "man's work." Some women themselves flinch and draw back at the mention of power: "I don't need it or want it; that would make me an angry person demanding my rights."

We women often believe there are only two choices: Bury your thinking, speaking, and doing (in other words, your substance) or be incensed to violence, abandon your spouses and families, take up a sign and march. Why have we been convinced that those are our only options?

I would like to redefine the playing field and allow a new option to emerge, because neither of the two choices listed above leads us to live authentically. The first denies the reality that we matter; the second demands that others recognize us so that we matter. The validation of self-worth comes neither from within nor from God.

In addition, neither choice represents a healing relationship with anger. Perhaps looking at the realities of what has happened or what is happening in our lives *will* move us to anger. We must recognize that there is a place for it. But, in the words of a wise Benedictine nun, "Anger can be a trap for us. It is like a door we must pass through as we see the injustice women have suffered. However, if we keep going through the anger-door, something is wrong."[2] We must face anger to open the door to a different future for ourselves and those around us.

We need to learn to be honest with ourselves and with God about our lives—the struggles, hopes, angst, and disappointments. If these realities become buried, they keep us from living a full and rich life. It stops up our prayers, disconnects us from others, and leads to a drab, flat way of life. We are just getting by, but not living restored, renewed lives.

A common reality for many women when relating to men is trying to be "less than" to please. We think that if a man really saw our desires, hopes, dreams, longings, fears, he would run in the opposite direction. A former boyfriend once presented me with a cartoon of a woman and man on a date. She is saying, "Ummm, I am thinking, that if you don't mind, perhaps, if it's okay . . . maybe, you would like to . . . " He handed it to me and said, "This is you." I was afraid that if he knew I really liked him, he would leave.

Before marriage, my dating policy was "diversify to reduce risk." Whenever possible I tried to get to know as many men as showed interest. Like a mutual fund, that seemed to provide heart protection. The daughter of a financial advisor, I took my father's policy on the stock market and applied it to my dating life. I tried to protect myself from the inevitable disappointment and failure that dating seemed to ensure. Or so I thought. Luckily, a good man came along and challenged my self-protection. He told me, while I was trying to keep him from getting too close to my heart, "Those same walls you put up to keep yourself from getting hurt are the same walls that keep you from being loved, cared for, and taken care of." My wall of resistance melted and I broke down in hopeful tears. They were tears of relief. I realized that I didn't need to keep working so hard to keep myself safe. Here was a good man who would honor my heart; he also wanted better things for me than even I was willing to dream. He overcame my defenses. He asked me to be with him in who I was, good, bad, and indifferent. He knew that real life and true love meant seeing each other's foibles and being committed even on those days that his wife would be an utter mystery.

Men and women are not only different in terms of physical traits but also soul design (which we will examine more in chapters to come), so we will always have different ways of perceiving or experiencing life. While difference can create tension, the power of an honoring man can redeem and restore broken places of a woman's story. So, too, is there power in a loving, healing woman's gift of herself to a man.

Mary, as you might remember from the prologue, never wanted to focus on herself, yet she went through a remarkable personal transformation. Over the course of several months, even her appearance changed: She started wearing clothes that were fashionable and vivid enough to draw attention to herself, something she would have run from when we began working together. Mary also became more involved in healthy, reciprocal relationships with real friends, rather than focusing solely on people who needed something from her. She invited people in her life to mutual friendships.

By reordering her priorities, Mary put her family's needs in perspective. Instead of telling her son what he must do, she made herself available as a supportive and listening ear for him. He did eventually pursue his high school equivalency degree, because he decided it was something he wanted to do for his life, not just to please his parents. The most significant change in Mary's world came from her husband, Tom. He had lost his own dreams and had been unemployed for many years. He had been content to let Mary shoulder the burden of being the breadwinner and managing the home. Because of his own insecurities and self-doubt, he had drawn back from their two children. As Mary began to change, he realized he could not stay the same. She was honest with him about how difficult her life was without demanding that he fix it. Mary stopped telling

Tom what was wrong with him and how he needed to change; instead, she described her hopes for and delight in him as a man.

She found a way to speak of her exhaustion and inability to cope with life in a way that did not blame him. As a result, Tom felt a compassion for her that he had not known for many years. He spoke more gently to her and wanted to care for her. He became aware that he had used her "nagging" as an excuse to avoid being the man God called him to be. He realized that he needed to change, so he decided it was time to find work. He also began investing himself in richer relationships. After joining the men's fellowship at church, he made a connection that landed him a challenging new job. Tom's situation started to turn around as he related to this new woman in his life. A woman of healing has the power to transform the scenes of life in which she finds herself.

With men, many of us are afraid to enjoy life and ourselves because we may be too much for him, overwhelm him, scare him, or be hurt. There is often history to back up our concerns, but hope means we do not have to contain something about ourselves in the presence of men. We have to realize that true love does not mean taking on the "mother role" with the men in our lives: We can allow them to stand and fall—even if it affects us. We have the opportunity to believe in what they may become and hold out that vision for them. Besides, our true selves may delight and draw them to be even better men than before.

Difference Is Opportunity

Who is woman? Two wise philosophers responded to that question and came up with very different responses. Søren Kierkegaard believed women were strange, full of contradictions and complexities. They confounded him.[3]

Evidently, women are confusing and seem to defy all logic, rationality, and categorization. I have often wondered what was transpiring between Kierkegaard and the women of his life when he penned this insight.

A different perspective is offered by Simone de Beauvoir. She wrote, "A woman is at once Eve and the virgin Mary. She is an idol, a servant, the source of life, a power of darkness and she is healing presence and sorceress; she is man's prey, his downfall, she is everything that he is not and that he longs for, his negation and his raison d'être."[4] de Beauvoir captures the "otherness" of woman for man. She describes woman as man's confounding mystery and yet the answer to his heart's deepest desire. These varied reflections deal with the complications and yet possibilities of getting to know who woman is, both for herself and for the men her life will impact.

You Hate Me; I'll Hate Me

Both secular and Christian counselors agree that women's greatest struggle today is with self-contempt. A person who feels self-contempt doesn't believe there is anything within to value and of worth for good. Why do women hate themselves? There is blame at their feet as well as at others'. Women's jealousy of each other is one form of harm, but realities of cross-gender struggle also shape women's self-understanding.

Many theology students are surprised by the writings of the early church fathers, in particular by their views on women. Although these men have contributed much to our understanding of the church, biblical interpretation, and doctrine, their ideas about women's virtues lacks some of the New Testament sensitivity that Jesus and Paul offered. Many of these writers placed full blame for the fall on Eve's naiveté and vulgar seduction, even accusing her of having sex with the serpent prior to her beguiling of Adam. The following quote illustrates their disdain for women: Origen stated, "What is seen with the eyes of the creator is masculine, and not feminine, for God does not stoop to look upon what is feminine and of the flesh."[5]

If only these restrictive views were held in a distant time and place historically. Unfortunately, many churches' policies today give women the same message: We are naive or we are a seductress. In either case, we are not to be trusted. Either we are innocuous, weak, and small or we are too dangerous. Instead of sensing men's fears and, therefore, considering their concerns as coming out of those fears, a woman often rushes to agree with them and discredits herself. She is all too willing to hide, retreat, make herself small, and swallow her words.

In this place of bondage, a woman will often express a real sense of fear. This happens when she refuses to be honest about herself or others. This fear has many faces. One such face is that she cannot be needy because she fears that no one will answer her. Living with unrequited desire feels impossible. Even Proverbs tells us, "Hope deferred makes the heart sick" (Prov. 13:12a). Another face is that she believes she cannot be weak or else she will be taken advantage of, and may repeat her story of being a victim.

For many of us, it is easier to assume a mask. It is more comfortable, at least on the surface, to adopt others' view of who we are. We let others define us. However, this is a form of hiding that only furthers our self-hatred. I worked with a group of indigenous people on an island in Alaska. Theirs was a community with a terrible tragic secret: For generations, the girls had been victims of incest. A high school teacher stated that every girl was incestuously raped by a member of her family by the age of sixteen. The most damaging element of this tragedy was that the older women did not protect the younger women from incest.

They even resisted social agencies' and churches' efforts to change the structure.

How could this be so? Likely, there were many reasons. We can imagine some of the older women saying, "We had to put up with it; why should these young women have it any differently? Besides, if we say that what is happening is wrong, then we have to face the horror of our own stories and deal with the harm we have known." It is easier in those cases to assume the mask, believe what family members might tell you is right, and stay hidden. Perhaps an underlying fear is, "If I were to remove the mask, who would I see there?"

The truth is that despite their mutual abusings, men and women need each other. We need the other and their difference from us to know ourselves. By listening and being willing to enter the other's story and life experience, we come closer to bridging the gap and learning the male experience, and they come closer to learning ours.

All women experience some form of oppression due to their gender, or even sexual assault, which can include rude comments and looks as well as unwanted advances. It can even occur vicariously through media or magazine portrayal. The ad slogan "sex sells" has serious repercussions for women. When women and their bodies are sexualized, it ensures that women will become victims through the fantasy of pornography and physical or verbal assault.

Every woman has been objectified at some point. A male coworker finds ways to bump you in the rear end or graze your breasts as he hands you a file. A leering neighbor tries to watch as you come home and turn lights on in your house. On a date, a boyfriend purchases pornography and wants you to look at it with him. Each of these scenes represents an abuse not only of your femininity but also of the purity God invited you to enjoy. It is hard to celebrate your femininity when others see it as an invitation to become a target of exploitation.

Will we believe what others say about us or will we believe differently? The hard part of choosing something else is that we think our only option is to become angry. There is another way: the path of suffering. Can you enter another's pain and heartache? You likely can't do it very well until you have entered your own.

Sorrow versus Anger

Over lunch, a good friend, who is African-American, and I discussed books we loved and things about which we felt passionate. The conversation drifted toward the injustice of life. We spoke of the different persecutions we have faced. Elements of our created beings had been dishonored in numerous ways, and we discovered that we had varied responses to situations of feeling ignored, discounted, or slandered. As Christians, we are called to offer a voice, advocacy, and care to the oppressed. Yet I had wrongly presumed that we needed to bury our anger and take the suffering life brings without question. Our conversation opened the way for me to reconsider my view of becoming angry over injustice.

Am I trapped in anger because I live in a sin-scarred world? In response to injustice I have two options: to harden in rage or to recognize my pain and weep. The first option is anger, but an angry heart can become one of stone. As the living organ of the heart hardens into that of stone, nothing can flow into it, and no streams can flow out of it. It is a closed-off, walled prison.

In contrast, a heart that tastes anger but refuses to stay there, that instead moves toward suffering, is an organ of life. Into that heart blood can flow. Inspiration, compassion, and spiritual wisdom pour forth from a source beyond the self. It also has the capacity for outflow. The suffering heart can give, pump on another's behalf, bleed, and still remain alive.

What price must I pay for a living heart? What is required of me to keep my heart from hardening and petrifying? The necessary element is a soul willing to sorrow. The price is immense—it is our lives. If I desire to care deeply for the sinful people around me, I must accept the reality that I will be hurt and disappointed. In light of this, will I risk naked tears of sadness on their behalf, or will I refuse to love because the cost is too great? Will I feel the weight of their sin so that, in my grief, I might serve the broken bread of Christ to them in communion? Can I live out grace in a way that can nourish a lonely soul?

In the midst of life's agony, who will be my advocate? How can I handle bearing the scars of a wicked world in my flesh? Christ, the mediator of God's glory to us, understood this call. He was nailed to a tree, mocked, jeered, and humiliated, to show us the way of suffering—the way we are called to follow. As he hung on Calvary, absorbing death in his limbs and our sin on his shoulders, he laid aside every right for us. He had the right to divinity, to justice, to angels' ministrations, to humble his accusers with the power of a justified, vengeful God. Yet this innocent, condemned man remained silent. He did not demand that people hear him; he did not assert his pure, divine voice. The words he spoke were those of forgiveness to his revilers and of promised glory to the thief on the cross.

Sorrow has the opposite effect of anger. Anger hardens, constricts, and closes off our arteries. Sorrow softens, cleanses, and creates a space to embrace the sufferings of others.

When we face the dark terror of reality, we can see the hurt and harm of this world. We can taste the bitter cup of abuse, poverty, oppression, loneliness, and fear. We can perceive the dark clouds behind the eyes of a friend. We can hear a cry of distress in the sigh of a stranger. Are we willing to hear, see, and feel the reality of others' pain? Are our eyes and ears open to God's words? Are we willing to face the reality of what Christ bore on our behalf? When we enter the darkness of life's struggles, we enter the enemy's inner chamber. Our call is to take the light of God's good news to that place. Although we may only have a lit match to cling to, and the dark night sky looms over us, this is the moment we are called to respond to with faithfulness.

The man of sorrows walks ahead of us. To know truth, we must be willing to drink Christ's blood and consume his flesh with fellow sinners. We must be willing to lay our lives on the altar of worship.

Will I carry the cross Christ has gently laid on my shoulders along the Via Dolorosa? I know the end of this journey can be no less than the despair of Gethsemane and the exposure of Calvary. Am I a willing sacrifice for God's glory and gracious purposes on this earth? When his angels come to send me out in service, will they find an open heart awaiting a commission, or will they find a sightless, deaf, dark heart closed to God and others?

As I left the restaurant that day, I felt a deeper call to choose sorrow over anger. My step was lighter because I recognized that I am not trapped in my response to life on this earth. The choice is compelling, but the courage required to move toward a bleeding, giving heart is more than I can possibly muster on my own. I am inescapably drawn to the gospel, because I know it is the only path to experiencing a sorrowing heart for myself.

At times we will rage in response to suffering. Of course, anger is a part of suffering, but it should not have the last word. We're meant to pass through it on the way to somewhere else. The question then comes down to how we respond to oppression and others' fear of us. How will we handle being abused, hated, and misunderstood? Will we grieve or rage? The answer we give will shape our stories and souls.

Biblical Witness

The Woman of Ill Repute (Luke 7:36–50)

According to Luke's account, a certain prostitute entered a Pharisee's house to offer a gift to Jesus. One might assume this house would have been strictly forbidden for a woman of her social standing, given that Hebrew society viewed her as "unclean." But this unnamed woman entered the house and wept on Christ's feet, kissing, caressing, and drying them with her hair. She likely let down her hair for the purpose of this visit. She ended this act of devotion by pouring perfume on his feet. This was an act of cleansing and purifying his feet, even preparing his body for burial. But it was also a highly sensual act. Was this a picture of a healing woman? Certainly, Jesus himself spoke of the significance of her action, "wherever this gospel is preached throughout the world, what she has done will also be told, in memory of her" (Matt. 26:13). She wanted to offer the finest parts of herself to this man from whom she felt strength, forgiveness, and kindness. Her tears were probably not something she had shared with the many men she had known—they were an intimate aspect of who she was. Although she knew very little intimacy and saw herself as spoiled and misused, her generous and broken heart was sacred. It was set apart for higher purposes. In her enjoyment of who Jesus was to her, she created a moment in which he could enjoy her.

This brave, extravagant woman was able to act in strength. She must have known that other men might have thrown her out, mocked her, ridiculed her gift, tossed her on the street, or even abused her. Many women might have chosen to avoid the possibility of that kind of shame and mistreatment. That which could have been a place of weakness became a place of courage. What gave her the confidence to pursue this risky act? The only possibility is that this woman walked in courage because she had tasted the power of Jesus' love. His love gave her the strength she needed to be a woman restored to beauty, and even innocence, in his presence. We are told, "Jesus said to her, 'Your sins are forgiven. . . . Your faith has saved you; go in peace,'" (Luke 7:48, 50).

She is given a chance for a new beginning. We, too, have this opportunity. Because we know the ultimate good man, who was willing to die on our behalf, we can move with a redeemed strength that is only possible through love by faith.

Study Questions

What are my experiences with members of the opposite sex? Do I see men more as weak or macho than thoughtful and protective? Why is that?

Are there some examples of redemptive men in my story who have helped me grow and know myself better as a woman?

In what ways have I believed the negative things people told me about myself?

Do I tend to express my anger or keep it buried?

How do I feel about experiencing sorrow?

In what ways would I like to be extravagant in my love for God?

3

Women to Women

The women I work with speak of a common theme: Women don't seem to enjoy themselves. Part of the reason for this is because we are afraid of the fallout in relationships around us if we were to do so. How will other women handle it if we show our own enjoyment?

Many times we experience negative reactions to our own enjoyment, whether of life itself, others, or ourselves. One such woman, Linda, called her friend and, in the course of the conversation, mentioned that she was proud of something she had accomplished. This surprised her female friend, who thought it sounded "bold." However, Linda quickly followed it up with, "Well, it was only secretarial work." Why did she draw back from being seen as pleased at the work of her hands?

Sadly, too often women like Linda draw back from expressing their enjoyment. This takes place in a number of ways. We are ashamed of our hopes, dreams, and desires. We try not to sound proud or seem too smart. We try not to stand out or be noticed. We hold back that which is the substance of who we are. We only offer what others seem to want of us. We want to be seen in ways others might like us. We shrink back from making others uncomfortable, saying things that might separate us from relationship, and expressing our sorrow and our anger. We shrink back from standing tall in any sense because that could mean that others will leave us, speak poorly about us, or not know how to handle us.

Relationships are far too important for most of us to risk damaging them on account of ourselves. We would rather keep peace and fellowship than enter the danger of being on our own. We fear being alone and isolated. Most of us have tasted enough of loneliness to want to avoid it at any cost—even, at times, at the cost of ourselves. As we continue to deny a place for our story to matter, our voice to be heard, and our souls to be significant, there seems to be less and less to the substance in us. In terms of our ability to speak, we scarcely know where our voices have gone, or how to retrieve them.

Restoration of Hope

Rachel was a top student in her class and had known years of teasing for being the "brain" and the "teacher's pet." Because she excelled in her studies, other girls were jealous and picked on her for not sharing their looks and priorities. Rachel was miserable. When she received early acceptance to an Ivy League school, she wanted to hide under a rock. She tried to keep it a secret at school, but a teacher, an alumnus of the university, revealed it to the class. Rachel knew the teasing and cool indifference of her classmates would only escalate. She felt so lonely and isolated. Why didn't those popular girls want to include her? She felt that she would have traded her smarts for an attractive figure and a football player boyfriend anyday.

Things had not changed much for her by the time she sat across from me, a confused, lonely thirty-something: "On some plane, I would gladly trade all my academic achievements for one moment of knowing I fit in and that I mattered. I still remember those mornings at the bus stop, listening to their giggles and seeing them standing in a tight huddle, close and warm, while I stood alone, praying for the day to end. I guess it was one of those mornings that I gave up hope of ever fitting in."

Her decision to lose hope was made with quiet resolve, but it soon began shaping her soul and story. Rachel relied on books for friends and shut down her need for people. She became an avid reader of Ayn Rand's novels. She emulated the architect in *The Fountainhead* who seemed beyond emotion, care, or concern for how others perceived him. *I am like him, truly free,* she thought. Through college, graduate school, and into her career, she was seemingly content to be alone, live alone, eat alone. Rachel did not appear to have any need for relationship. Or did she?

Sitting in my office, glancing thoughtfully out the window, she confessed that she had needs. She had been so effective at shutting down her heart to others that eventually she felt as if it was closing in on her and choking the last few breaths of life out of her. Rachel's isolation slipped into depression. From there it was not long before she no longer wanted to live: "What am I living for anyway, the microbes in the petri dishes that I work with? The late nights in the lab when everyone else who has a life has gone home? There has to be more to life, or why live?" Rachel faced the hard questions of existence that all of us confront if we have suffered with integrity. She questioned:

"Does my soul matter; is there a reason I am here; can I know who I am apart from relationship with others?"

In the process of our work together, Rachel began to open up to relationship. This began with me as her counselor and then proceeded to a few growing friendships, and even dates in the months that followed. Rachel recognized the fact that being human meant not only being aware of her needs relationally but also not losing hope in God, herself, or others.

Back in her high school days, the bus stop resolution built a wall around her heart that effectively kept out the hurt but also kept out the joy, promise, and possibility of being known and knowing others. Rachel needed other people. She needed to be loved and cared for, and she needed to have others do likewise. She was not the Lone Ranger or Ayn Randian character she tried to make others believe she was. Rachel needed others, but she also needed God. In parallel fashion, as her heart shut down to others, it also closed off to God. In the process of our work together, she began to see that a desire for relationship was foundational to hope and life.

Like Rachel, many women feel their hardest battles come not from the men in their lives but from other women. The shame of the bus stop, the playground, or the teams at school etches a deep mark in our souls that can take a long time to overcome. What is it that makes relating as a woman to women so challenging?

Expulsion from the Sacred Circle

Most women I have spoken to have a scene in their story that takes place on a dangerous playground. We all had it somewhere. One of mine took place in sixth grade when I was expelled from the "cool" table. I didn't carry that event around in my conscious memory. In fact, it was a story I had chosen to forget and buried successfully, or so I thought, until a comment was made to a friend of mine four years later. The girl said, "Do you think Heather still hates me? Well, I still thinks she dresses like a baby." When my friend told me about the incident, it was as if I had no clue what she was referring to, but then all of a sudden a bright, blinding light came on in my head. I knew exactly what she meant.

I was sitting in my sixth grade classroom at the front girls' table, not the back table reserved for the "misfits" or mis-fitting ones. I knew several of these popular girls from the year before, so I assumed my place at the head table. The ringleader decided to bond the group through finding a scapegoat. These girls were all dressed in T-shirts and jeans—the only "proper" attire for a suburban public elementary school. I, on the other hand, wore dresses and saddle shoes (obviously before they were recycled as "fashionable"). This made me an easy target. I tried to grin and bear it. I took my father's advice, "Don't give them the satisfaction of letting them see you cry." I tried to become a rock. As the kicks under the table, elbow jabs, notes telling me to die, and finally Scotch tape in my hair continued, I decided to concede defeat and go to the back table. Although several of those back table girls had difficult home lives, they were much more welcoming and kind than my previous deskmates.

The tape in my hair was the last straw for me. My passive teacher cut it out of my hair while never addressing the warfare taking place right in front of him. I suppose I realized there would be no justice nor advocate to help me. I had been expelled from the "sacred circle" of friendship and was not sure what it would take to be included again. This was one of my shaping stories, particularly in regard to dealing with other women.

The Safety of Confined Spaces

In times of exclusion and rejection, we search for comfort and security. In our fear and fury, we will gladly accept little boxes as new places to call home. After all, they look safe—granted, I can't speak, stand up, or breathe, but at least I seem to belong. These boxes can represent the binds we get in by being only what we're supposed to be or do as wife, mom, businesswoman, friend, church worker, daughter. . . . We flex and bend to conform to the ever-expanding expectations of others in our lives. It is as if we whisper, "I'll be or do whatever you need, just please don't leave me alone!" Or even deeper still, "If people really knew the extent of my heart, the undulations, confusion, madness, temptations, rage, even rapture, could they stand me? Will I be cast out of the playground?"

This search for security can take on sinful means to achieve its aim of inclusion. We comply, compromise, and agree to worship false goals of security, status, and snobbery to remain "in." These ways of relating derive from the pressures of life. Life's options and possibilities seem overwhelming. However, each decision involves loss: Choice means that a yes to one is a death or no to all the others. At times, this may account for what is known as our feminine fickleness.

It is common knowledge among students of female psychology that women fear success because it separates us, sets us apart, and opens us to loneliness, isolation, attack. It is much more pleasant to blend in, fit in, and be approved of by the crowd. There are plenty of voices telling us how to fit in, from advertising campaigns to the latest self-help books, talk shows, and television programs.

What is true between the genders is also true among same sex friendships: We need, yet destroy, each other. Our most powerful weapon is our tongue. Scripture warns of the dangers the tongue can present to people of faith. Our words form an identity for ourselves by inclusion and exclusion. We cut down another person to be accepted by others. Gossipers feel powerful in the secrets they share, mindless of their murderous intent.

We avoid telling the truth about our affections and day-dreams for fear of being abandoned. Women learn to temper themselves, to be more palatable for others. We try to be careful, which leads us to be "care-filled." We assume if we are restful or angry, that might disappoint others. It could be too risky to be where we are because we could be "out" as a result.

Most women have, at one time, been excluded by a female monopoly through cutting down and competition. We were not allowed in the sacred circle of childhood, and we can ever after strive to return to the inside. Some will pay any price for inclusion: plastic surgery, cruelty to others, the right clothes, cars, and zip codes. With other women, we often seek belonging over being. When we conform to fit the crowd, we prevent our and others' enjoyment of our uniqueness. When we act out of fear of being alone and losing relationship, we live with a refusal to trust in others or God.

Biblical Witness

The Woman with an Issue of Blood (Mark 5:25–34)

What is the price of standing alone? In his Gospel, Mark tells the story of a woman who spent years isolated, shut out from social circles, and considered an outcast. Because Jewish law decreed that women were unclean when they bled, her bleeding excluded her from normal relationships with others. She lived as an outsider. Something in her knew that the new man who had come to town was different. With him, things changed and were transformed. What was old became new. Broken things were restored. He offered a new vision, new words unlike those of the rabbis, about God, love, seeds, the kingdom. He was known as a healer. He was gracious and willing to extend his hand to free an imprisoned soul. The blind saw, the lame walked, the demoniac became sane—this man could work miracles. What compelled her to believe that he would extend this healing power to her? She may not have been sure that he would, but perhaps she thought that if she could only get close enough, she might reach out to him. Surely, if he exudes healing he wouldn't notice, particularly in a large crowd, that her small hand had connected with him, that she had borrowed some of his strength to mend her broken body and lonely heart.

She was taking a risk. She was forbidden to enter a public setting like that because others viewed her as infectious, unclean, perhaps even contagious. What if someone recognized her? They would shame and revile her. What if this teacher, Jesus, knew who she was—would he treat her any differently? True healing, the possibility of being restored in body and to community, was worth all risk. She had faith enough to cast herself into an unknown future, depending on a God who was larger than she knew, but who she hoped could be true. She risked everything to seek a new level of life enjoyment that God might have for her.

Jesus did the unexpected. He stopped, turned, and spoke to the crowd. "Who touched my clothes?" (v. 30). Her bleeding had been instantly relieved, but just when she thought her plan for redemption had worked, he caught her. What might he do?

Not content just that she receive physical healing, Jesus wanted to make her healing a public event, so she could be known as a woman restored, healed, made new. Her heart must have known much relief to receive such a gift from the one who knew her soul, story, and substance. Her touch mattered to him. Her healing and her status in the community mattered to him. He announced her healing for her and invited her to celebrate and be celebrated.

Jesus was sensitive to her as one well acquainted with his own places of loneliness. Jesus knew about being left alone. This is captured not only on Gethsemane but also in his many moments of being misunderstood.

There will be places we will go on our journey that no one can go with us, through the deaths of loved ones, disease, possibly even depression and despair. No one can travel the road of life through to death for us. It is good to have people in our lives, but fundamentally, the cross we have to bear is an individual one (even in community). This was my overwhelming impression while I was standing on the Via Dolorosa in Jerusalem—Jesus' path of sorrows or suffering. He walked the road to Calvary with people watching, jeering, perhaps flogging him; one person assisted him with his cross at one point, but he was profoundly alone. I was reminded on that cobblestone road that, being people of the "good news," we must be prepared to face times of loneliness.

The question for us is, How will we handle isolation? Will we despair, as my client Rachel did, or trust God? The first choice is depression, shutdown, and withdrawal. The second choice opens us to mystery, the unseen, and God in ways we never dreamt possible—but it is risky. The foundation we believe is secure will be radically shaken.

We may be called to give voice to our story and to let our substance show—to take as big a risk as the woman with the issue of blood. It requires remembering our whole stories, not just a sketch but the full-color scenes. I can recall the abusive comments of the girls at the "cool" table in sixth grade, but I avoid describing the color of the saddle shoes and dresses I wore that were the objects of my shame. Why? A part of me would rather not reenter the agony and weight of that place. I would rather not feel the loneliness and rejection again. In my heart, I know I have a choice. However, to choose life and hope, I know it is important for me to confront the fullness of the story. I know that when I choose to take the road to restoration and freedom that Christ offers, I must face and narrate my brokenness and the boxes that bind me.

Scenes of fear, powerlessness, and loss are hard to tell. I know this to be true in my own life and have seen it time and again in the privacy of my counseling office. Being women of healing not only involves feeling free to stand tall but also encouraging the women around us to do the same. We can risk being our own person for the sake of something greater than group acceptance: God's presence can mean more than "what is pleasing in humans' eyes." We remember our stories as we re-member our substance to be a worthy offering to our redeeming God.

Study Questions

What are the unique challenges I have encountered in my relationships with other women?

How have I been shut out of the sacred circle of childhood?

What are the boxes I have chosen to live in rather than risk others knowing and potentially rejecting me?

What are the moments in my story when I have been restored to community? What were they like?

What stories about me would I rather other people not know?

4

Stories of Difference

The theme of difference appears in varied forms throughout our lives. It occurs when we relate to members of the opposite sex, friends and enemies, strangers and foreigners, people and places. Like a contrasting color backdrop that shows a scene more clearly, difference invites us to see ourselves. We are welcomed into relationship with another and, through that experience, discover other sides of ourselves in the process. The following stories illustrate what it is like to be known, misunderstood, or challenged as an outsider. Opportunities to encounter difference surround us, if only we have the courage to step into them. It may be risky. We may be changed in the process.

Encountering Difference

One Thanksgiving Day, while surrounded by fine cuisine and close friends, I had a conversation with a woman I had just met, a Muslim from Iran. She had recently moved to the United States with her new husband, leaving behind her home and all that was comforting and familiar to her. She found herself in the midst of a strange country with bewildering customs. With sadness, she said, "Had I known the cost of forsaking my homeland, I might have made different choices." She spoke of her family, with whom she had lived until she was married. In her home, she said, meals were a central part of their lives, a place where loved ones lingered for long hours, sharing the small events of the day, telling old stories (which only got better the fourth or fifth time around), and reveling in the consolations of friendship.

While she was talking, I found myself beginning to look with different eyes at the scene surrounding us; the turkey, cranberry sauce, and pumpkin pie were different from the lamb and couscous that formed the basis of her cuisine, to be sure, but it was more than that. I realized that this was probably as close as we ever get to the celebration of family that this woman was describing. And even the phrase "celebration of family" seems to have a hollow ring in a country where infrequent family gatherings can be seen as an obligation rather than a place of reunion and comfort. I found myself longing for something that she had to offer—the opening of doors to another land, one I might never see nor be welcome to enter, yet one that elevates certain values that resonate in me. In a few short hours, I experienced a radical reversal. For me, her homeland had always conjured up images of hostages and people fleeing a government that hates all I represent as an American. As she spoke, I realized that our culture of instant gratification, convenience, and individualism was far more hostile to her way of life than I could have imagined. As my husband and I drove away from that evening and the conversation lingered in my thoughts, I was aware that I might never get to Iran. However, through her eyes and her story, I was brought close to her homeland, which created an echo of dislocation and hunger in my own heart: It was the gift of receiving another culture.

Being a Foreigner

Most people have experienced being "Other." At some point their status was that of alien, foreigner, outcast, exile, rejected, or unpopular. The following are a couple of my stories of being Other.

During my junior year, I studied abroad in France. I found this a significant challenge despite nine years of study and being a French major. As a college student, I felt naively optimistic that I could get by during my six months overseas. It wasn't until I got into the taxi out of the airport and tried to give instructions to the driver that I realized I could not speak the language. I could have discussed French art, history, and existentialism with the driver but not my directions to the hotel. Despite months of studying and living with a French family, I never seemed to achieve more than an eighth grade level of language proficiency in terms of being able to communicate my inner thoughts, struggles, and desires. They were patient with me when I fouled up grammar and syntax or chose a more common word to describe something important. I could tell that they viewed me as less intelligent, coherent, and capable. I could not communicate my heart. Because I could not command the language, I felt bound, misunderstood.

While living abroad I tried to find experiences outside my experience as a Westerner: I wanted to travel to a place wholly other. I had the opportunity to travel with some other students into preliberation Prague in 1987. Without any idea what we were going to encounter, we went to the Czech embassy in Vienna and applied for "vacation" visas.

As we approached the Czechoslovakian border, I regretted that we had not told anyone we were going behind the Iron Curtain. Machine gun–armed militia lined the track, dogs went through the train, bags were inspected, and rounds of questions were asked. I thought of the Bible in my bag; it had been my closest friend during my six months overseas. Before we reached the border, I had resolved I would fight if anyone tried to confiscate it, but when I saw the lineup, I realized the situation was definitely out of my control. It was then I became aware that no one knew we were in Eastern Europe. At that point, I realized that if they wanted the Bible, they could have it. Maybe it would do them good. I would gladly surrender whatever belongings they demanded as long as it did not mean my freedom.

As we toured the city, it became clear that we Americans did not know the rules of whom to speak to and whom to avoid. Most buildings had surveillance cameras, and some official-looking people took our pictures on the streets of Prague. No one spoke English, and the few who spoke to us wanted to change money. Most people refused to look into my eyes. From my outsider's point of view, it seemed they did not look into each other's eyes either. Any of you who have lived in a city know this to be a reality: Eye contact is a little too close for comfort. I was an alien, a foreigner. The situation felt out of my control.

If you are like me, you have known moments of being alienated, but you have also been guilty of alienating others. In overcoming the discomfort of dealing with someone I do not understand, I can make them Other and thereby dismiss them.

What the Other Has to Teach Us

There are two realities to Otherness. One is negative: Others are used as scapegoats, to unite a group against a common enemy, to give a sense of worth over and above someone else, or to find an excuse for why life does not work as one group feels it should. In these situations, we choose to make someone Other out of fear, because we feel threatened. This can happen on playgrounds, by the office watercooler, and in political campaign headquarters.

The second truth to Otherness is positive: There are benefits not only to having Others in our lives but even to being Other. Others provide windows into our own soul and story. We deepen our knowledge of our God, our doctrine, and ourselves when we are questioned by difference. Others serve as a mirror, providing clues to our real selves as they reflect our hearts back to us. Are we willing to truly see an Other? Will we allow the Other to impact our fragile structure of avoidance? If we dare to see others more as subjects, less as objects, we might be able to give and receive authentically. To do this we need to recapture the scriptural adage, "speaking the truth in love" (Eph. 4:15).

At times, refusing to love, we can become rigid fundamentalists like the Pharisees that Jesus criticized. There are moments when, refusing to speak truth, we can be anemic relativists afraid to offer something of the substance of who we are. How we offer truth is critical. Loving words do not shame. They are not about demanding and persuading someone of what is right or wrong. Words spoken in love trust that God is at work in the other person; words spoken in love betray our willingness to witness to the truth in our own stories. Since God's grace is irresistible, we can trust he will do more with our offering of loving words than we can ever hope to achieve on our own.

Difference provides us with an opportunity to enter mystery—it is a place where we are less in control than we might otherwise choose. In that place we are invited to trust God in the midst of a larger, more frightening world. Here we are reminded of our call to act, serve, and hope for others who have been strangers but can become friends.

How to Bridge the Gap

There are two ways to overcome the gap between "us" and "them." The first is through the genuine offer of relationship. What does it mean to listen intently to another without looking for a place to contradict them or insert one's own opinion? Henry Wadsworth Longfellow said that if we knew our enemies' secrets and stories, their pain and suffering would defuse our anger toward them. He invites us to see beyond the surface story that our enemy presents to discover that they are human, like us, and have shared life's joys and sorrows. The hope is that we can muster curiosity and not be too hurt to try.

The second gift follows from the first. We need to learn the other's language. Not only a foreign tongue but what they mean by what they say. Does it mean something different than our first impression of their words?

Barriers of language and misunderstanding can be overcome. A poignant example of this happens in the film, *Amistad*. Spielberg, as the film's director, offers an insightful example of the power of language to redeem a situation. The film tells the story of a ship of Africans brought to America to be sold into slavery. There is a mutiny, and the slaves take control of the ship, but they are captured and tried in a New England court. At this time, the issue of slavery is raging in the United States and threatening to tear her apart. The issue on trial in that New England courtroom was whether or not these men and women were free or born slaves. If they were born slaves, the Americans were permitted to sell them into slavery. The defending counsel needed to prove that they were free. Unfortunately, the language barrier made the Africans appear distant, foreigners, perhaps as just slaves to the Americans.

Cinque, the leader of the Africans, has testified and told his story through an interpreter. The defense attorney is now questioning a member of the British armada to verify Cinque's story. At this pivotal point in the film, Cinque chants softly, at first, but then builds to a yell, "Give us us free! Give us us free!" He had learned enough English to be able to communicate and use his adversary's tongue to bridge the gap. Up to that point, the language divide had not been adequately crossed. Once it is, it changes the story. You can tell by the music that Spielberg is trying to hook you, to tell you this is a climactic point in the film. Spielberg's use of dramatic cinematic and musical effects tell the viewer, "This is important; do not miss it."

The moment the bridge is crossed, it redefines the Africans and their situation. In this scene, in what was supposed to be an open-and-shut case because the judge has been pressured to render a "slave" verdict, that dramatic moment changes the outcome and convinces the judge to declare them "free."

In the next scene, a picture Bible has been given to the Africans. This scene lays out a detailed description of a suffering God who died and is resurrected on behalf of others. It goes on to show how the Africans identify with him. I find this scene very hopeful. Spielberg demonstrates that to make sense in someone's life the gospel story has to speak their language.

Today it is the poet, novelist, filmmaker, and journalist who tell us stories that make us feel, hear, and see the plight of others. They take us to places where we can, in turn, bring hope and healing. They help us focus on specific, everyday cases of cruelty and make us see and feel the humiliation and suffering that we inflict on others.

Others May Surprise Us

To relate well to the Other, we need to genuinely respect the Other. This is challenging when we are confronted by difference. The word's definition says the Other is not like us. But respect arises out of the other-centered love that is at the heart of the gospel. Perfect love casts out fear enough so that we can love others in revolutionary ways. As you will be able to tell from the next story, there are plenty of times we are not living out fearless love, but God graciously decides to use us anyway.

A few years ago, I learned a powerful lesson on a bus in New York City. A homeless woman entered the bus. She was speaking in a loud voice, addressing her comments to everyone and no one at the same time. As luck would have it, she chose the seat next to me. Her cries became shriller and I, like the other passengers, attempted to ignore this intrusion. I contemplated jumping from the window but decided that might be a bit extreme, and I was not sure I would survive the drop on the other side. Perhaps with God's grace, I could handle this moment. I breathed a prayer, aware that fear and discomfort were truer of my heart than love for this woman. However, as I reached in my purse, it occurred to me I could offer her a mint candy. I was going to have one anyway; why not see if she would accept? It felt risky. What if she increased her volume and made me more dramatically her target?

I pulled out the roll of candy and asked, "Would you like one?" She paused and then accepted the offer. She immediately stopped talking. For the rest of our ride together she was silent. Both of us sucking on our mints, we shared a moment of peace. I doubt the mint had anything to do with it. Perhaps my small gesture was an acknowledgment, "You are here, and your life is intersecting with others' lives. Some of us, in our braver moments, might even see you or speak to you." There is power in treating one another as human; she gave that to me by being the peaceful recipient of my small gift.

A wise theologian, Anthony Thiselton, writes, "A love in which a self genuinely gives itself to the other in the interests of the other dissolves the acids of suspicion and deception. . . . giving the self to the Other in love and serving the other's interests as one's own remains ever fresh and creative, in that it builds."[1] Those are powerful words of opportunity and invitation.

Loving the Other Is Costly

What we do with the Other tells a great deal about us. I recently had an experience that I am confident I would have responded to very differently in the past. I was flying alone. Sitting next to me was a woman who, like myself, had lots of paperwork on the tray table in front of her. It was hard not to notice, as we sat right next to each other, that I was reading and preparing from my Bible and her set of forms was labeled in bold letters, "Planned Parenthood."

There are two things you need to know about me to understand the implications of this discovery. First, in my counseling practice, I have done a fair amount of postabortion recovery work, and second, my husband and I have struggled for years with infertility. Given those two issues, I said a quiet prayer, "Lord, you've put me here for a reason. But I am hoping and praying that you don't want me to do, say, or be anything in this moment." My reluctant mood was more like, "Let this cup pass from me."

However, as providence would have it, in no time at all she turned to me in a warm way and asked about my work. I told her I taught in a seminary. She asked what that was. I realized that she did not know much about my world, so perhaps this was my opportunity to offer her a different picture of the Christian community than she might have previously encountered.

When I asked her what her profession was, she said she was a nurse practitioner at a women's health center. As we continued the discussion and she described her interest in the women that came in to see her, I said something that felt very genuine. I told her it must be good for those women to have her care for them. She was warm and kindhearted. I wanted to offer her words of love. I could not erase from my mind the faces of the women whose sorrow I had shared or the cries of my heart for a child. It felt important to keep these two, love and grief, in tension, rather than try to straighten her out on the realities of when life begins and argue issues of morality or legislation, as many Christians I know might have done.

She inquired about my counseling practice and asked whom I counsel. I mentioned one area in which I work is postabortion recovery. I waited to see if there would be any follow-up response. She was quiet.

As she and I deplaned, I said a silent prayer: "May I have loved this woman today in such a way that she will be curious and not afraid of the Christians she will encounter in the future. May that curiosity lead her to a curiosity about this gracious, redeeming God we serve."

Jesus heard the cries of outcasts, sinners, the powerless and weak. Scripture shows, through Christ's compassion for the lowly and downtrodden, that who we are and what we struggle with is of vital importance to our Maker. We do not have to look far in Jesus' varied encounters to see his hand of compassion, words of consolation, and looks that banished shame to know he saw the individual in the moment. The experiences of Mary Magdalene, the woman with the issue of blood, once-blind Bartimaeus, and the honored host, Zacchaeus, bear testimony to Christ's grace-filled presence.

By being Christ-like, we can offer others a spirit of inclusion in our welcome and our prayers for them. One church I attended for several years was involved in the search process for a senior minister. In the interim, the younger associates had their chance to preach. After listening to the eighth sermon in a row on 1 Samuel—each sermon accompanied by at least one football illustration—I realized I felt overlooked. There were no stories with which women could relate unless they were hardened sports fans themselves. Instead of just sitting there, angry and frustrated, I had to ask myself, *Will I pray for those who overlook me?*

How we welcome, pray, sit at table, and invite others to join us says much about the state of our own hearts. Do we continue to see ourselves as redeemed sinners, living every day dependent on Christ's death and resurrection on our behalf, or do we think we have it all together and that those Others need to get it right? I am grateful to God that it is not all up to me to succeed at loving well. Christian love is costly. It requires more than we have to give; it exhausts us so that we run out of our own abilities in order to rely on God's grace alone.

As we conclude our discussion of difference, I invite us to love in radical ways that are costly. Let us expand the table of welcome and inclusion. May our eyes see and our ears hear the voiceless, the alien, the nameless, the exile, so that the stranger might become a friend, so that as we listen they may hear the irresistible call of a Savior who cares so deeply for our Otherness that he came down and chose to be Other with and for us.

Biblical Witness

Ruth (Ruth 1–2:12)

Ruth was important enough to the salvation story that Matthew included her in Jesus' genealogy. The Gospel writer could easily have skipped over her name and focused on the men who were the backbone to Jesus' Davidic and Abrahamic heritage. But Ruth mattered; so did the other three women mentioned, who all happened to be outsiders to the Hebrew people. They were foreigners, and yet God, who spent much of the Old Testament calling his people to remain pure and to avoid intermarriage with Gentiles, used these very women in a mighty way.

Ruth chose the harder path. She decided to abandon her homeland, her people, and her community. Instead of knowing how to get around, whom to trust, and where to find the supplies she needed, she decided to leave it all behind her in Moab. She chose to care for her grieving mother-in-law, Naomi, and to create a new life. Not only did she choose to make Naomi's people her own, she also agreed that Naomi's God would be hers. Ruth was a risk-taker. Stepping into the unknown required great courage. She was no doubt aware of what abuse she might encounter for trying to join a people known for their separateness from other races and religions. She must have known she might be misunderstood and mistreated by those who would see her as an alien.

Ruth's story is that of an outsider who came into a new community and was able to change her own life and the lives of others as a result of her inclusion. Instead of hiding her face and not interacting with the people of Bethlehem, Ruth acted on behalf of her own and Naomi's welfare. Boaz, a man of importance and a generous heart, took a risk as well. He was willing to take in a foreigner and place her with his servant girls, who collected what the harvesters left behind in the fields.

In the face of his kindness, Ruth asked him, "Why have I found such favor in your eyes that you notice me—a foreigner?" In essence she was saying, "I am different and alien. It is not customary for you to extend your care to those who are not of your family or your people."

Boaz credited her with the sacrifice she made to care for her mother-in-law—the leaving of homeland and parents to "live with a people you did not know before." He pronounced a blessing upon her that because of her deeds she might be richly rewarded by the God of Israel "under whose wings you have come to take refuge."

Boaz did not realize that this God had a plan for her protection and care that would directly include him and his future lineage. God's comforting wings are broad enough to enfold those considered outcasts, other, alien. The good news is that God's grace includes all of us, even those we are afraid to risk loving.

Study Questions

What are my stories of being an outsider and foreign?

How have I excluded others and viewed them with distrust because they were different?

What emotions surface when I consider risking speaking to someone I might ordinarily avoid making eye contact with during my day?

Have I felt the discomfort of trying to relate to and love people who are different from me in their values, attitudes, politics, and lifestyle?

Do I have any hopes of trying to offer others something more than I have in the past?

5

The Place of Beauty

Is there something of beauty that reflects the heart of a woman? The word *beauty,* at times, is used to describe cosmetic lines, but it can also be used of God and the deepest levels of awareness and existence. In his statement, "The soul that beholds beauty becomes beautiful,"[1] the ancient philosopher Plotinus was saying that it is important for our soul to grow and deepen in beauty. In the following stories we will explore the correlation between who women are, who they are called to be, and this elusive word "beauty." Through them we will search for some common threads to women's encounters with, and love for, beauty.

Beauty Lovers

Homecoming

Now that my siblings and I are adults, when we return home, often from quite a distance, a warm welcome awaits us. My mother will seat us in the dining room on embroidered seats—ones we always feared spilling on when we were young. She sets the table with fine china, crystal, and silver from generations ago. At each place setting there is a little gift or note. In the center of the table stands a floral arrangement. As we enter this scene, our raucous voices soften. We sit a little more gingerly than we might normally, our manners improve, and we feel a sense of dignity imparted by just being one of the fortunate guests at this table. Stories are shared, invariably with laughter, and the meal is savored. No one rushes to push back their chairs from the table. That family meal is not just food for hungry bodies but an experience of communion and creativity.

In this fine meal, pleasing not only in smell but also visually, beauty is offered. A fine meal is an aesthetic, sensual experience.

This doesn't just happen, of course. Important feasting tables have to be prepared. The upper room was readied for the most profound meal ever eaten. The essential elements were present: the bowl and towel for foot washing; the bread and wine for blessing, breaking, sharing, and storytelling. And we tell that story now and for generations to follow as we gather at God's table. It is fitting that our churches center on a table.

Greek Life

Those who have had the opportunity to wander through the halls of a sorority house on the grounds of most universities and colleges will find an interesting similarity in how they are laid out and maintained. Those who have witnessed not only the interior of a sorority house or hall but also that of a fraternity know that quite a contrast can be drawn between the two. The difference is palpable, not just in appearance but also in smells and sounds.

There were thirty-five fraternities and seventeen sororities when I attended the University of Virginia. I joined a sorority. The interior had curtains, carpets, attractively colored furniture with matching pillows, and pleasant paintings on the walls. In some regards, one could have mistaken it for an attractive hotel lobby.

On the other hand, next door and along our road stood the male fraternity houses. I helped my younger brother move into his fraternity room at the start of the school year. What I saw there continues to haunt me. This fraternity, like others, had a certain odor. I had the distinct impression that everything had been left out too long or never should have been left out in the first place. There were no paintings, carpets, or curtains. The house had the feel of a trashed, abandoned house, not a place ready to receive tenants. My brother's room was considered the "trophy" room in the house because it was the scene of ongoing warfare with a neighboring fraternity. The other house would frequently fire rocks through the windows, so most of his windows were punched out, and glass lay shattered on the floor. As he was to find out, this was considered normal. Why was there such a disparity between the ways the college women and men chose to decorate their surroundings? Does it point to a difference between the genders?

It's not only fraternities and sororities, though. It seems that churches cater in different ways to each gender. For example, note the difference between a women's banquet and a men's breakfast. The women's event would most likely offer tablecloths, china, silver, perhaps even crystal stemware, with attractive place settings and centerpieces.

The men would probably use paper plates, plastic utensils, napkins or possibly paper towels as substitutes, and sit at bare tables.

Gatherers

Rob Becker is a comedian who has taken his comedy routine to Broadway and traveled the country with his sidesplitting show, *In Defense of the Caveman*. He examines the differences between the sexes and the mystery that is woman. He points out the different ways men and women shop by describing a visit to the mall. He believes that men go to the mall as they would go on a mission or a hunt in caveman days: They go, see, kill, conquer, and buy that red sweater. Women, on the other hand, are easily distracted, and what started as an errand to buy a certain item turns into wandering, gathering, touching, and feeling different garments and textures. He suggests this tendency is due to cavewomen's responsibility to gather the fruit, berries, and grasses that were ripe in season. They needed to be attuned to color and detail and be able to scan across a vast horizon in search of fruit.[2] Could Rob Becker be suggesting that beauty is innate to a woman's soul?

I believe that women are good at sensing detail. At times this means we can lose sight of the big picture. We are aesthetically aware. We notice color, shape, patterns, designs, and presentation. We are aware that we are capable of creating a moment, a scene, even a life of beauty. First Peter 3:4 speaks of the beauty of one's "inner self, the unfading beauty of a gentle and quiet spirit, which is of great worth in God's sight." Scripture invites us to let our beauty serve others. Song of Songs is a wonderful feast of beauty.

Simone Weil, a French Catholic theologian, wrote, "Beauty is eternity here below."[3] She implied that we catch something of heaven in our perception of earthly beauty.

She went on to say, "If beauty were to be made real, it would sweep all secular life to the feet of God."[4] What those words suggest is that beauty draws worship. If beauty were really real, made concrete fully, secular life would find God's invitation to be irresistible. Our souls are drawn to beauty as an expression of God's persuasive call.

The Dark Side of Beauty

The story does not end with our standing before beauty with clean hands and hearts. There are downsides to beauty. On this side of heaven there are other realities to our experience and enjoyment of beauty.

Fresh Flowers

External beauty is fleeting, temporal. When I was in my twenties, I did not like to receive cut flowers—there was something about receiving fresh flowers that depressed me. The beauty and the smell were wonderful, but for how long? Three, maybe four, days. Then the flowers began to brown and wither. They would die. It seemed wasteful to cut them from the ground for a few days of pleasure. This dislike may have been founded on the demise of several dating relationships that seemed to coincide with browning roses. Somehow a houseplant seemed safer. I would wait all year for those blooms to come, but the quick death of fresh flowers unsettled me. Beauty this side of heaven quickly fades.

Sistine Splendor

My husband and I had the opportunity to travel to Italy several years ago. We stood in front of the Sistine Chapel with hundreds of other pilgrims who had waited for hours to step into this marvelous space. I had been there fifteen years earlier, but there were noticeable changes. Michelangelo's *Last Judgment* is painted on the front wall. When I had originally seen this fresco its background was black, but now it was restored to its original bright, bold, sky blue. It is so brilliant one feels lost in the color and the busy scene set upon it. We stood there, staring, with our necks strained from leaning back to take in the entire ceiling of frescos.

I was aware of a struggle in me. Part of me wanted to turn and walk away immediately because I knew that eventually I would have to do so. I could not stay in that place. There is something about beauty and its temporal nature that created in me a longing and an ache. I desired something that I could not get hold of or hold onto. Eventually we all must walk away.

Think of the beauty of a wedding day, or a moment of rich connection or reconnection that has left you hungry and desirous, wanting more. With beauty comes an ache.

Beauty Thieves

Another downside to beauty is the danger it can cause for us. Enjoying beauty and story means also being willing to live in our ache. Jealousy can be a way of escaping our longing. Beauty's danger is that it draws jealousy—a bitter pill likely all women have experienced at some point. Envy surfaces when we are dependent on others for our sense of self-worth. Someone else has beauty that we do not seem to have; therefore, we will use gossip as a weapon to deface or disfigure her. The emotions argue: "If she is less, then I may be more."

When I was in fifth grade, I was friends with a tough girl in the class. She was outspoken, some might say obnoxious. I liked a boy who did not like this friend of mine at all. One weekend, I spent the night at her house. I do not recall if this boy had called me before or since, but somehow he ended up calling for me at her house. After answering, my friend told me to get the phone. I did not realize that she hadn't hung up her phone and that she was able to overhear our conversation. She was jealous that a boy would be interested in me. I remember telling him that my parents were out of town and that is why I was staying with this friend. It wasn't true. Likely he found out where I was from my parents. Obviously, I had not thought this out too clearly. Needless to say, my friend heard the entire conversation. When I hung up, I heard her crying in the bathroom. I felt terrible. I can still recall leaning on the side of the sink, looking at her tear-streaked face in the mirror, and telling her that I was so sorry and did not mean it, but realizing I could not take those words back. They were out and had done their damage. That day I marred her beauty. I put down who she was as a person to protect my own self-interests. I did not want this boy to think less of me or my attractiveness because she was my friend. She chose to spy on me and take something from what this boy was offering me. We both sinned against each other.

A conviction was birthed in me that day: Beauty is dangerous. I realized I had significant power for evil in another person's life. I became determined to avoid ever harming another with my words. I became fiercely diplomatic. My husband is not all that fond of this characteristic. If he asks me whether something he is wearing looks okay, I respond, "yes, it is fine," or "it looks interesting," which is not always an honest answer. This story is one in my life that has shaped me and left an indelible imprint. I knew I could wound with my words and disfigure beauty.

Beyond being jealous of beauty, we may also choose to absorb it from others. We want to control it in others, so we attempt to absorb their passion. In relationships, this comes out through manipulation, control, or intimidation.

It can also appear in a variety of internal forms. Eating disorders are an exercise in control or misuse of food and one's body. We also use beauty illegitimately when we obsess about our looks. Vanity functions like cotton candy: We think it will be nourishing to pride ourselves on outward beauty, but, in fact, it is empty.

When we desire beauty but know it fades, we can even exercise cruel means of extracting it from others. A manipulative woman assigns parts to the people in her life, demanding their conformity. They lose their own identities and become appendages to her drama. She will use backbiting, praise, even punishment to keep her friends in their places. The last thing a person who consumes beauty wants to face is how hungry they really are. They rush to the next fix, obsessing over their appearance, grades, clothes, or purchases. Unacknowledged hunger leads us to addictions.

We desire relationships, but when we want to absorb beauty we can become controlling. As the saying goes, our greatest area of strength is also the place of our greatest sin. Many times we end up killing the very thing that feeds us. A woman with anorexia carefully monitors every calorie. She plans her life around food and exercise, and yet this very preoccupation is slowly killing her. We desire relationship, but find ways of sabotaging to ensure that people will not want to be around us.

Part of our inner battle involves our refusal to forgive others for wrongs inflicted upon us. What has been done to us informs who we are; most of us are not fully free from past wounds. If we cannot forgive, we can become paranoid. We become afraid of others; our suspicion keeps us painfully alone. Underneath isolation there remains an ache, an unfulfilled desire for the beauty that relationships reveal in us and in others.

Beauty is fleeting. Destroying or devouring it can't keep or secure it. There must be other ways of dealing with beauty.

I believe it is possible to step into the ache as opposed to away from it. The battle of being beauty thieves leaves us weary. We crave rest, but we are afraid to sit in the ache left from not having eternal beauty. What keeps us from moving into the emptiness of unfulfilled wanting is that we fear that God will be silent in the face of our cry. Simone Weil said, "There are only two things piercing enough to enter our souls, they are beauty and affliction."[5] Both point us to something greater and call us to an unrealized purpose. Both stir our longings as foretastes of what is to come—beauty by way of fulfillment, and affliction by way of relief. She claims that in our pain, we share of Christ's sufferings and partake of his relationship with the Father. Often, we are met with God's silence in response to our crying out. She claims that silence is God's answer: It is the response he gave his Son on the cross.[6] Perhaps silence is not being ignored by God but being profoundly met by him. It is Jesus' cry echoing our own. It requires faith to consider that silence might be presence. If that is true, then there is an opportunity to rest even in the midst of our pain. At that point, silence is almost a place of rest.

We can choose how we will handle our own soul's desire for beauty. We don't have to ignore or try to control it. We can choose to honor that part of us as a reflection of what God may have for us to enjoy in heaven. We can enjoy moments, scenes, and experiences of beauty while appreciating that they won't last. In the wake of beauty's loss, we have the opportunity to listen for God and await his return.

Biblical Witness

I like to imagine what might have been in the mind of Esther as she wrestled with her choices.

73

Esther's Musings (Esther 4:12–17)

For such a time as this. What will the king do with my audacious request? Who am I to demand the favor and attention of the king? I am but one of his many wives. But, on the other hand, how can I sit by and let my people be persecuted because they are different and because their faith is a thorn in the side of the power-hungry Haman? I wish I had no standing and that my fate were not to be inside the walls of the palace. I would like to do nothing and trust that God would raise up a prophet, a deliverer, a man. Why me?

I suppose that other women of faith have gone before me: Deborah, Miriam, Sarah. But usually there were men, Barak, Moses, and Abraham, to be alongside them to support the choices they made or to make the choices for them. My uncle Mordecai has warned me and invited me to take action, but he stands outside the gate. I am alone in this place. And yet a nagging line keeps running through my troubled mind, *For such a time as this.* [This was part of Mordecai's response when Esther had him informed of the danger of approaching the king.] Could it be that this is true for me? Am I here now for a reason, even though I am not a man? I have some power, more than the village women from whence I came, but I am still a woman alone in a man's world.

For such a time as this. If I am to take this step forward, how am I to convince the king that he should deign to hear and receive me? I know I am taking my life into my own hands. He could be too tired to raise his scepter, or annoyed and choose not to protect me. Other women in the harem would not dare be so intrusive. Would he consider my act on the level of disrespect that cost the last Queen, Vashti, her position and reputation? But I know Mordecai has gathered the Jews in Susa to fast for me. As these three days pass, and I and my servants fast, the inevitable draws near. I must carry out my promise to my uncle and go to the king, even to my death.

For such a time as this. What is the plan needed to carry out my mission? It is important that I invite the king to consider well my proposition, especially knowing it will mean going back on his word. I must find a way to entice him, draw him in, and honor him. I will go before him dressed in my finest royal robes and use that moment to gain favor to invite the king and Haman to not only one banquet but two that I will prepare for them. Once they have been in the presence of good wine and food, I will put my request before the unsuspecting Haman. I will ask King Xerxes to spare not only my life but the lives of my people. I will identify the one who is proposing harm against us, and the king will need to choose between me and him. I go forward in faith that my people's God will strengthen me and allow my beauty and that of the meals I create to be used for a higher purpose.

Study Questions

How do I feel about the concept of beauty?

Does beauty draw or repel me? What do I dislike or distrust about it?

How have I tried to take beauty from others? How have they tried to rob me of my own?

When in my life have I felt called by God for "such a time as this?" What is it like to recall that scene?

6

The Gift of Sight

What do women see, and what do they refuse to see?

Janelle's Journey Back to Life

"I have spent my life running, trying to numb myself, and you are asking me now to stop and take a look in the mirror. That feels impossible." Janelle wrinkled up her brow and made a sickened face as she tried to convince me that feeling and thinking about her own life situation would definitely not be therapeutic for her. I was aware of her thick walls of resistance toward the process and toward me for suggesting it. We were stuck. I knew no other way to invite her back to life than to ask her to listen to the pain of her children and the hurt in her own heart.

It had been several years since Janelle had been in communication with her children. After their father's death, she had done her best to raise them as a single mother. Her long periods of depression meant that she had spent much time lying on the couch while her children did the cooking and the chores. Because of her chronic worries, she had been on antianxiety drugs. She had found the medication helpful but began abusing drugs and alcohol. There were sections of her life that were blank and, as far as she was concerned, irretrievable.

As adults, her son and daughter had fled to different cities and would go years without letting her know their address or phone number. They might send an occasional card but without a return address. Clearly, they did not want her to find them. When Janelle's daughter turned thirty, she sent her mom a note indicating she had contracted a life-threatening disease. The note read, "I guess I have not wanted a mom for a long time, but now I know I need one. Could you come and be with me in this?"

Janelle was confused by the note and aware that she did not know what to do, so she decided to find a counselor. "Frankly," she told me, "there's a lot of my story I don't want to remember, and I don't see how that is relevant to the question before me. Should I go and be with my daughter, or should I write her an angry note about her neglect of me over the past decade?" I had responded, "What do you want to do?" She had no response.

"There's a chance I might see my son. He could come to the hospital. They have kept in touch despite both ignoring me. What would I say to them? I know I haven't been the best mom, but I tried to do right by them. I remember how when Sally went off to college she came home and yelled at me for not being there for her. I had to have five whiskey sours that night to go to sleep. What an ungrateful louse. And now this. I don't know if I can handle having one of my kids die. Granted, they have been half dead to me as it is, but I guess I always hoped one day things would be patched up and we could all go back to being a family. Maybe if I just ignore it, it will go away."

Janelle had an inkling of hope for a reunion with her children and, ultimately, a restored relationship. It was this hope that eventually led to her growth and change. She was conflicted about the work that was needed to rebuild something with them, and whether or not they would take her back into their lives. She knew that to love them in the present required looking at the damage of the past and being honest about her failures and theirs. Ultimately, she chose to see her daughter's note as a request for her mother's blessing and for peace between them. It was not too late after all.

See, Hear, Feel No Evil: A Refusal of Sight

When I first entered graduate school, I wrote a poem that expressed an awareness of how I operated in the world of relationships. My eyes were beginning to see. It is called, "That's very much really me."

> Really me is talking
> saying I don't need you
> you're not here now anyway
>
> I'm just fine
> I'm okay
>
> Really me's not scared
> Really me won't cry
> feelings are weakness to the strong they say
>
> Life is good
> I'll succeed

Really me runs every race
smiles at every face
tries to please everyone but herself

Really me's such a very lonely
very nobody place to be

In the process of self-discovery, I was aware I had chosen ways of living that were soul-numbing and based on denial. There are many ways that we refuse to see ourselves, including self-deception and abdication. We abdicate ourselves when we give our power over to others in order to preserve harmony. Being powerless can still be a form of control; they call it passive-aggressive for a reason. By not being truthful about our lives and who we are, we are setting ourselves up for two of the most common female struggles: depression and anxiety.

One woman in my life has a frequent refrain of, "No bad news! No bad news!" This motto guides how she relates and what she chooses to see of the reality of life, struggle, and suffering.

There are many things that women refuse to see. We do not want to see the issue of change, yet our very bodies are full of change within each month and each season of our lives as women. Within our own body we go through all the different periods of life: before we can conceive, when we can conceive, and then menopause and beyond. We are bound to change through seasons and cycles, but we don't want to. We try refusing to change and this causes bitterness, depression, and worry.

Teen anorexia has been described as a girl's refusal to become a woman: She avoids the physical changes of puberty by not giving her body enough nourishment to develop and sustain her cycles. She does not want to go through the change. For whatever reasons, becoming a woman is considered negative, so she attempts to maintain a boylike body. The price of womanhood is too great—too much may be required of her as a woman.

Change involves loss and requires grief. Grief is something we work very hard to avoid. Not many people want to feel the heart pangs of absence and emptiness. Grief can offer healing, but at the time, it feels like we are going through a death. However, it is the death of what was or will never be that opens the door to new life. We refuse to see because it involves change and loss, which, in turn, invites grief.

Our Harm

We also refuse to see both our own and others' harm. Our harm is the way we punish others for the fact that life is not working the way we want. Some women with whom I have worked have seen themselves as nothing more than victims: "If I am a victim, then isn't it true that my sins don't count?" If you are nothing more than a victim there is no need for repentance or for a Savior. There are certainly moments women are victimized and need to recognize that they are not responsible for the harm perpetrated against them. But there are also times when we use our pain as a weapon to harm others. Deeper questions remain: How will you allow that experience to shape your story? What will be true of your view of yourself in the future?

If a woman perceives herself as without power then she needs to manipulate to get her way: "If I have no power to act as your equal, I will have to try to go around the back and try to get someone to do something the way I want it done." In my marriage, my husband is saddened and angered when I subtly try to get him to do what I want. Instead of just asking him for something outright, I use manipulative words, which are rather comical since he sees right through them and does not appreciate them at all. This is the downside of being married to another counselor. "Wouldn't you like to fix the screen door today?" That is not what he would like to do. In fact, he does not even like the screen door, so why am I asking him to fix it as if he would want to do it in the first place? I wanted him to do things my way, and I tried to slyly encourage him to think it was his idea in hopes that it would sweeten the deal. I may have seemed timid in my request, but my desire for control was evident. I am learning to ask him directly for what I want rather than trying to get him to own my desires for me.

Women have been known to manipulate in ways other than with words. We can also manipulate with our bodies. That is the oldest trick in the book. For centuries, it was a woman's only way to exercise power over men. Scripture provides us with numerous examples: Delilah saps Samson of his strength using the tool of seduction. The adulteress described in Proverbs 5–7 lures to death. She is the opposite of Lady Wisdom, who is attractive and winsome and leads toward life. We can speak of something that stirs desire or is irresistible as drawing us or others, as calling us in a certain direction. For example, Ruth used her sexuality for good—good for her mother-in-law, the community, and for Boaz when she drew him to be more of the man he could be as her kinsman-redeemer. She was willing to offer herself to the honorable Boaz, who respected her request and secured a future for her lineage.

This leads us to the question, What is good sexuality? Song of Songs gives us hints. In this book, we find that sexuality is about desire and abandonment, pain and pleasure. It arouses longing and delight. Both male and female are praised for their beauty and sexuality. Wonderful mutuality is present in their gift of body and soul to one another. It is difficult for us to bring this intriguing book to our sex-saturated culture. It finds little place to stand because we are aware of our tarnished hands and dirty hearts as we stand before such a raw, vulnerable book.

Our society has taken the body, particularly the female body, and used it as a tool for arousal, particularly in advertisements. In college, I studied the appeals of advertising and what they were trying to elicit from their viewers. I was given a men's shaving cream commercial to interpret. On this glossy page was a tall, fluffy mound of shaving cream. If you looked at the foam for more than a few seconds, you could see that naked female bodies were swimming throughout it. I was not sure how the naked females connected with the shaving cream, other than perhaps the promise that by using this cream, naked women would flock to you. It was evident the bodies were there to stimulate the male viewer into purchasing the product. The use of sex to sell is so pervasive that we've become blasé about it. It is as if, like this subliminal ad intended, we no longer "see" it.

Given how misused the body has become in our culture, we have ceased to care. At times, women become co-conspirators by using their feminine wiles to entice others: "If I am going to be treated as an object, I might as well use my good looks or curves to get my way. Some call it 'sleeping your way to the top.' I prefer to think of it as asserting my fair advantage. We women have to do something to even the score." There are other ways we acquiesce: "If I am with a group of men who start telling dirty jokes, I tell my own. I want them to know I can keep up with them and can handle whatever they dish out." We also offer our bodies in exchange for security, comfort, or assuagement of our loneliness.

We can draw life toward us like Lady Wisdom, or attract death like the adulteress (Proverbs 1–9). The choice is ours. It is very hard to live out a redeemed sexuality in our culture today; we are up for incredible challenges when we try. Are we willing to see the ways we draw others to death instead of desiring something better for them and for ourselves?

Others' Harm

Not only is our harm something we refuse to see, but there is another category as well: others' harm of us. In earlier chapters we have examined how others' harm can come from both men and women. An abused wife recounted to me:

> In time I stopped wondering if I was being abused. I noticed that as soon as he started yelling I could find a safe spot somewhere deep inside me that he couldn't reach; no one could reach. There was a place where I was safe. I was never sure how long the screaming continued. I watched his mouth moving and was able to shut out the sound of his voice. I stopped thinking anything was wrong with how he was treating me.

We adopt several postures to stay alive in a world that is fallen, a world that does not appear to have our safety and well-being in mind. We can assume the stance of being naive: "If I am naive, it might not cut so deeply, or at least I don't have to feel it, so I will be immune or seemingly immune to the harm of others." This is an assumed numbness, but it doesn't set us free. We begin finding we are sleepwalking through most of our life. One author put it this way, "There have been so many things I hadn't allowed myself to see, because if I fully woke to the truth, then what would I do? How would I be able to reconcile myself to it? The truth may set you free, but first it will shatter the safe, sweet way you live. . . . a woman in deep sleep, goes about in an unconscious state."[1] There is something about refus-

83

ing to see the harm others bring that is numbing, that puts us to sleep.

The price of sleep is great: We lose any sense of connection to life, ourselves, others, and God. The challenge is to decide what is necessary for coming awake.

There are consequences to shutting our eyes and refusing to see. If we refuse to see, we can neither speak the truth nor feel reality. We live delusionally, that is, we believe what is not true. Supporting a fantasy world requires a great deal of energy. If we are working to support something that could collapse upon us at any moment, we can never stop, slow, rest. Therefore, we go to bed with lists running in our heads. These lists may awaken us in the middle of the night and prevent us from returning to our much-needed sleep. I wonder, what might we see, feel, hear, and think if we stopped or paused this motion?

My body is often closest to being overcome by an illness when I get a burst of energy, a last gasp to do work, clean the house, move the furniture, or rearrange my life. That is just when I am about to collapse. My body refuses to rest even when it needs it the most, maintaining my delusion at all costs. We justify our busyness because it seems purposeful. I try to justify my busyness by contending that perhaps I was serving someone else—maybe even God— and therefore I had to do x, y, z. It is interesting how quick I am to overemphasize my place in the kingdom. Am I afraid that God's will would not be done if I were not quite so active?

If we refuse to see, we're caught spinning in a cycle of motion. All this activity leaves us exhausted. Common questions we ask ourselves in the midst of stress or burnout include: Why have I gotten to this place? Why is it so out of control? Why do I seem to stay here? Why do I make myself stay here? These are important questions. Notice that most of them have an air of helplessness or hopelessness about them. This is true if our hope is in ourselves.

Our vision needs to be greater than bouncing in and out of burnout.

We have a choice as to what we will do with our exhaustion. Many of us have lives that are full to overflowing as busy moms, wives, Sunday school teachers, lawyers, activists, daughters, sisters, and friends. We are pulled in multiple directions simultaneously. We are the ultimate "multitaskers." At the end of an exhausting day, week, or decade, it is not uncommon to hear women crying, "I am everything to all people at all times and yet nothing inside at the same time. I have lost myself." We live in denial when we do not see how exhaustion robs us not only of life but also of the ability to know and worship God. We pretend that life is manageable and we can control our universe. We rush farther and faster to prove we have what it takes to flawlessly overcome the realities of a fallen world and protect our relationships. But then a crack emerges in the pristine image we create, and the increased activity catches up with us. Perhaps happiness is not found in busyness alone.

There is an alternative. We can learn to be people of the Sabbath. The Sabbath was God's decree to his people to call them to a place of rest, relaxation, and worship. God knew the importance of resting after the hard labor of creation. God, as an infinite being, modeled the power and necessity of rest for us mortals. We are designed for rest. No wonder our bodies protest when we do not allow ourselves a chance to slow down and catch our breath.[2]

I have spent years studying the topic of rest and Sabbath. It is a practice my husband and I have incorporated into our weekends. We are intentional about not working from Saturdays after 5 P.M. through dinnertime Sunday evenings. As good Protestants, it is important to us that this practice not become a "work" but rather a place of receiving God's good gift of rest. When we are unable to keep our Sabbath, we are grateful for an opportunity to remember we are people that need grace. I encourage you to find a way of practicing Sabbath that works in your life as an outworking of thankfulness, not an obligation of faith. Many writers describe mini-Sabbaths they take throughout a day or a week as moments of pausing, breathing (literally), remembering God's goodness and faithfulness, and resting with a mood of thanksgiving.

My study of rest has led me to interesting places in Scripture. Several years ago, my husband and I were in a Bible study that decided to tackle the complex Book of Ecclesiastes. As we began studying chapter one, I noticed I was experiencing the text differently than the men in the group. I wondered, is my reaction unique to me, or does it reflect a difference in how women and men encounter this text? Over the years of teaching and examining this passage with students, the women students have had reactions similar to my own. Here are verses 4–9:

> Generations come and generations go, but the earth remains forever. The sun rises and the sun sets, and hurries back to where it rises. The wind blows to the south and turns to the north; round and round it goes, ever returning on its course. All streams flow into the sea, yet the sea is never full. To the place the streams come from, there they return again. All things are wearisome, more than one can say. The eye never has enough of seeing, nor the ear its fill of hearing. What has been will be again, what has been done will be done again; there is nothing new under the sun.

The men in our group immediately responded with moans, stating strong feelings of futility and hopelessness in their experience of Ecclesiastes' opening verses. Their mood was, "Why are we even reading this book? Let's stop. I can't stand it." The women were far less verbal initially. I was aware of a very different reaction stirring inside me.

I found these verses comforting and perspective-giving. They sounded whole. The idea of entering this cycle of life resisting neither the changes that it brings, nor the reality that life goes on and there is no end to the story, felt rest-giving like an experience of Sabbath. At the time, I was wrestling with grief and found these words reassuring. Perhaps they were saying to me, "This too shall pass." Instead of feeling hopeless, as my male compatriots had, I felt hope-found.

I am not sure my response is confined to my personal lens at the time. Without prompting, upon hearing these verses from Ecclesiastes, many female students have described them as "circular and soothing." This text said to me, "Stop doing so much and learn to BE who I have created you to be." In the end, my doing does not change the pattern of the sun, wind, or sea. God's ways are far more vast and mysterious than I can fathom, so God invites us to enjoy and live the moment.

To "be" is a challenge for all people, as Shakespeare so eloquently reminded us. For the women I have known, "being" is a central struggle for them personally, relationally, and spiritually. How can I be with God? Is my being with God enough? How can I offer anything to my husband at the end of a long day? What can I give my children in their many needs and demands? Will the man I am dating think being with me is exciting enough to want to stick around? The question of being is at the core of many of our choices and styles of living. Leaving these questions unexamined can lead us to adopt an exhausting pace. But owning and exploring these questions can recall us to God as our source of rest and inspiration (breath) for life.

There are times that life can be so overwhelming that we choose to close our eyes to see or ears to hear the confusion, pain, and disappointment that exists in our and others' stories. We try to shut off our hearts and live a numb, comfortable existence rather than ride the roller coaster of life's rough edges. But we need to see life and relationships as they are in order to be and to rest. They invite honesty and hope.

Biblical Witness

In the New Testament, we hear many accounts of Jesus healing men and women of physical, spiritual, and emotional diseases. Here is one such story that involves the willingness and invitation to see. I like to imagine what it must have been like to hear that the healer man, the awaited one, Jeshua—the one who saves—was passing by.

Blind Bartimaeus (Mark 10:46–52)

For many years I've longed to have what others have: sight, to recognize color, soil, people, shapes, and changes in light and seasons. I feel, hear, taste, and smell them, but my eyes stay closed. Could it be that the miracle man might walk out this gate of the city? I have hoped for so long that I fear disappointment. Please, don't tempt me with possibilities. My hope has grown dark. I fear trusting it into the light. This time could be the last. I am not sure I could handle the progression of sorrow to deadness and despair again.

Surely this Nazarene, if he made his way to Jericho, would leave by another gate. If he were here, I doubt he would see me in the throng of people crowded about. I can smell their warm bodies, hear the jostle and hustle of them pushing past others. I shake my stick and cup, hoping for a handout, for food. Without my eyes I am without means, wages, or usefulness. Would I even know if the Messiah passed?

A strange stir, like a growing rumble of thunder, burns throughout the crowd. I hear the rumor that Jeshua is in town and is heading this way, his sights set on Jerusalem.

I feel the crazy hope of some forgotten dream rally in my heart. I give it heed. I cry out.

The others around me rebuke my woeful call. They are revolted at the sight and sound of a desperate man. They mock my request and shun my selfishness. But if he truly is a compassionate healer, as I have heard, he could not turn me away as others have. The cry in my voice is muffled by fear of further judgment, disdain, and ridicule: The crowd has powerful control.

Yet something in me won't be silenced. I grow agitated. To sit in silence is to admit defeat. To speak is to risk everything on this stranger, this one whose ears may be as deaf to me as my eyes are blind. Will he even hear, then care, then come to me, a desperate, screaming fool?

Before I could stop myself, the cry went from my throat louder than anything I knew was in me, "Son of David, have mercy on me!"

In the silence of what felt like eternity, I sensed a stopping and heard a voice of truth and warmth, "Call him." The voice spoke for me, to me, in and through me. I began to feel a surge of life from deep within rise up to warm my whole being. I felt sure I was radiating light. His friends called out to me, "Cheer up! On your feet! He's calling you."

Stripping my shroud, the heavy cloak that guarded me from inclement weather and the arrows of abuse from the people around me, I leapt up and moved quicker than a blind man should toward the sound of the voice that heard and knew me. That voice chose to bring me cheer this day.

He asked a question that I had waited so long to be asked: "What do you want me to do for you?" Could it be this easy, could this stranger mean these words and deliver, no matter how great my response might be? I said strongly,

"Teacher, I want . . . I desire to see." In that moment of encounter that would forever rewrite the pages of my future, he spoke words that healed, blessed, and commissioned me. "Go, your faith has healed you."

The instant his words were spoken, I could see. His words tore the scales of darkness off my eyes and made a way for light to pierce me. It did. I reeled back as colors, shapes, and brightness invaded first my eyes, my mind, and then my being. It was too rich, vibrant, explosive, and shocking for a mere mortal who was comfortably familiar with shadow. It had been so long since I had seen the light. I might have been afraid had I not been so near this man of tender strength and healing voice. I will never forget his smile and his eyes looking into my eyes; this is the first face I have ever truly seen. This face will define all those that follow. This face had compassion on me and taught me to see. Are his tears for me?

I knew at that moment there was nothing I could do but follow this man as he turned toward Jerusalem. And all I want is to follow, to move toward this man and make his mission my own. I must offer no less to this man who has given me my new life and new eyes. I have been seen, heard, known, touched, and forever changed.

Sight may entail grief over the past and even the present, but it also invites us to rest and enjoyment. We are free with Bartimaeus to follow Jesus as the scales fall from our eyes and the face that defines all faces sees us. Jesus knows us, loves us, and died for us, to make us clean and new creations. He offers healing from darkness, misunderstanding, and a past story that may imprison us. Will we cry out? Will we invite God's healing touch into our lives that we might be women of healing as well? Only then can we risk seeing, stop running, and enjoy his Sabbath rest.

Study Questions

What are the good parts of me I don't always choose to see?

What are dark places in my heart that I avoid admitting are there?

How have I drawn others toward life rather than dishonor or death?

Have I numbed my heart toward others or toward God?

What would it take for me to "be" and rest rather than continue rushing in my exhaustion?

How has Jesus restored my sight? What new lenses has he provided?

7

Accepting Our Bodies

"I have finally come to the conclusion that no one sees my hips quite the way I do," said Liza, who had spent years battling issues of body image. She had been in and out of eating disorder treatment facilities as she worked hard to avoid facing the deeper issues in her life. These manifested themselves in extended periods of food abstinence.

Earlier in our conversation, Liza had told me, "The black dress I tried on was fitting. Oh, I hate fitting clothes! They make me uncomfortable. I am sure everyone in the clothing store was staring at my protruding hips. As usual, the friends who came shopping with me tried to offer their assurance. 'No, it really looks good.' 'It is not too snug.' Lines I have heard hundreds of times. But, you know, this time something inside me felt differently as they spoke. I realized I was not so quick to disregard their words. A strange thought popped into my head—perhaps my view is unique. I have finally come to the conclusion that no one sees my hips quite the way I do."

Liza sighed and smiled after this last statement as she acknowledged that she was turning a corner in her life, even though she was not entirely sure the future would be safe or secure. The eating disorder had promised, at least temporarily, some control over the chaos of her experience. What would she do without this to fall back on?

I have yet to meet a woman who does not struggle with some aspect of her physical appearance. Our bodies aren't picture perfect; models are quick to point out that even they do not look like their pictures in advertisements that have been digitally enhanced. Yet the standard has been set. Women have inherited centuries of censure in terms of how their bodies, clothing, makeup (or lack thereof) should be fashioned. From bound feet to liposuction, botox treatments to clitorectomies, the regime for the acceptable or attractive body is often painful, invasive, and confining. We are accomplices in joining the effort to restrict ourselves lest our feet grow too large to fit into Cinderella's dainty slipper. Is this really what God had in mind?

Part of the challenge is that many women have known times of not feeling confident about their looks or personality. Perhaps we were able, as children, to enjoy the beauty of life and creation; maybe then we felt pretty and loved. It is possible to recapture those places of promise and hope; yet learning to accept our bodies may be the greatest challenge before us. No woman I know likes all of her body. Why is this disdain for and discomfort in our own skin so deeply engrained in us? This is not to say that men do not share in the plight of not feeling their physique is "right." However, in my experience as a counselor, women's sense of diminished self-esteem seems more directly a result of their body type than men's is.

While working with several survivors of breast cancer, I learned of the powerful loss and grief these women feel after having their feminine form altered forever. Implants may offer some solace, but, with the risks involved, many women face the prospect of living with a constant reminder of what was lost. An identifying mark of their femininity has been removed. The breast they lost may have been a place of nourishment for their infants, and it certainly was a sign of coming of age as a woman—far more than a section of anatomy has been destroyed. For these women, their story and sense of self have to be rewritten, like a tapestry rewoven to include a new, painful band of color. They must consider all over again who they are as women.

Every year I have the privilege of working with second year, master's level counseling students in a training group. At times the group is coed, other times it is all women. In the women's group, the walls come down about the struggles of being women. Stories get told and retold about how we live out our calling as women and how we invite other women to do likewise. As part of our study, we read articles, short stories, and poetry.

One particular poem has assumed legendary fame through an annual group reading. This poem is called "Phenomenal Woman," by Maya Angelou.[1] Given the poet's life and experiences, this poem represents redeemed, embodied sexuality.

A few years ago, after we studied this poem together and discussed our individual reactions, one of the women insisted that we enter into the poem in a chorus of voices. It has a rolling cadence that we found fit well with group recitation. Moreover, we found ourselves practically dancing in a hope-filled chant by the end. There is delight in communally speaking the words of a woman's perspective on how special she is even though "she's not built to fit the fashion model's size."[2] This *phenomenal* woman goes on to recount how her self-possessed physicality is part of what turns men's heads and causes people to stare, because her beauty both exudes and invites. Our group found freedom to appreciate these bodies God has given us to inhabit. Perhaps God even longs for us to delight in and feel pleasure in our bodies—especially when our bodies refuse to align with the fashion model size.

How We View Physical Intimacy

Bodies are difficult to come to terms with because they invite us to experience sensual pleasure; our senses awaken us to see, taste, smell, touch, and hear. Although most would argue there is nothing wrong with our five senses, many Christians may feel hesitant as our discussion moves into the realm of physical intimacy. What do we do with teenagers whose raging hormones lead to inevitable temptations and desires for sexual experimentation? Perhaps it is hard to know how to talk about sex with youth because it is an arena that remains taboo even for most Christian adult discussions long after the wedding day. We live out the dualism between soul and body in our practice of faith. Throughout church history, theologians have wrestled with the place of the body in the religious life. What might it mean for believers to respectfully bring body and soul back together?

Historically, many thinkers have encouraged a mistrust of woman because she was seen as the corrupter of men's purity, the temptress and seductress. The other side of the coin is that woman has also represented untouchable purity. Women were either vilified or deified, with little room in between. It was a woman's body that lured men to give up their vows, abandon their thrones, and make foolish choices in pursuit of its possession. Perhaps this antipathy and suspicion has seeped into women's self-consciousness as well. Most women I know are uncomfortable with their bodies and their sexuality.

Some may ask, "Is it wrong to desire a man or an intimate relationship even before I am married? I have all these feelings, I don't know what to do with them. I try to tell my body 'no,' but it doesn't listen." Women have many questions when it comes to their experience of pleasure. Notice how the body in the quote above is disconnected from the person—the "it" that acts on its own. What do single women do with pent-up sexual feelings and desires? They could acknowledge their true longings and grieve the absence of fulfillment, but that is not usually the direction most choose. It is not sinful to acknowledge sexual feelings or physical responsiveness and accept that this is how we are wired. What we are responsible for is whether or not we act on our feelings. Living out our faith is measured in our choices in action. Many single Christian women choose to deny their sexual feelings, or they end up acting upon them, which puts them into a cycle of shame and self-punishment; they take these two roads rather than feel and grieve.

Physical love is meant to make us feel good and has inspired poetry; Song of Songs is one such example. This book, which early church fathers allegorized extensively to avoid any erotic overtones, became a favorite source for sermons for many church mystics. Bernard of Clairvaux wrote eighty-six sermons on this book. The mystics of church history write in extremely passionate and descriptive language about God and the delight or rapture of being found fully in him; they speak of union and oneness with God as a merging of the soul with its divine lover. Perhaps earthly love is meant as a mirror and foretaste for what love will one day be like between us and God. Indeed, the Book of Revelation tells us a great wedding feast awaits us, with the church as God's bride.

The decisions my clients make when it comes to pleasure often provide a window into their image of God. Is God a taskmaster, waiting for you to slip up and catch you? Or is God the one who created the Garden of Eden, filled it with all that could satisfy mortal desire, and invited you to enjoy it and walk in it with him in the cool of the day? Those are two very different images of God and his intention for his created order.

Because physical intimacy can be so threatening (both in and out of marriage) and, furthermore, is fraught with taboos, some people tend to avoid feeling any form of pleasure because it may parallel a sexual one. For these people, all pleasure is seen as wrong and sinful. They are motivated by guilt to maintain a vigilant abstinence from dating relationships altogether. Guilt also prevents them from enjoying other aspects of life, such as a walk with a friend, a delicious dessert, a beautiful sunset. An excess of guilt can even ensure that some people may find themselves in less than honoring relationships because of the belief that, "This is the best I can do, but at least I am not alone."

I often help my clients consider where the places of relief, rest, and joy are in their lives. I also pay attention to how they move away from places of peace and restoration. They might open themselves up to act on temptation, or they might be compelled to grow in holy ways that would require more of them in the future. Neither choice sounds safe to them initially—staying shut down seems wiser.

How We Celebrate Life

I watched eight-year-old Laurie scamper down the stage steps with an insuppressible smile on her face. She had just completed her first ballet performance. The little girls around her had been tense as the elementary school curtain raised on them in their stiff pliés; however, by the end, all of them were smiling and leaping freely. Laurie enjoyed knowing what she was doing and had fun improvising when she forgot. I was delighted to celebrate this event with her, but her excitement made me wonder at what age

97

little girls no longer smile at their own achievement and rush to their relatives with the words, "Wasn't I good?"

When a woman enjoys herself and allows others to delight in her, she often punishes or sabotages herself. This is easier than the ache, loneliness, and emptiness on the other end of enjoyment. She chooses numbness and deadness to guard herself from enjoyment.

During her high school years, Priscilla received high honors and became a National Merit scholar, but she did not want to tell any of her friends. Her fear of losing relationships prevented her from feeling pleased with herself. They were not good students, and she feared that they would be threatened by her achievements. They might make fun of her, and she did not want to be set apart. She had learned that standing out by acting pleased about something she had accomplished could set her up for rejection and disapproval.

Most writers on discernment and vocation highlight the importance of paying attention to what brings you pleasure in life. You may find God's call for you in the things he has equipped you to do well and enjoy. Not everyone takes pleasure in caring for infants, the elderly, the infirm, or the homeless. Your passion for this line of service may be worth listening to. As British runner Eric Liddell once said, "When I run I feel his pleasure." If a woman is afraid of experiencing pleasure in any form, she runs the risk of missing out on an important way in which God might choose to speak to her.

I often describe enjoyment to my patients as an invitation to put themselves in the way of a wave that they would like to have hit them. What might that look like for them? What risks would be present if they were to venture that far onto the beach? Maybe they will find they are strong enough to resist any undertow that threatens their convictions. If they can overcome the pull of their own ambivalence, which keeps them safe and dry, they may have a wonderful experience. Ambivalence is effective at short-circuiting our growth by keeping us aware of the emptiness on the other side of pleasure. It is easier to be depressed than to choose to step into what God might have for us. Although more comfortable, that choice will ultimately be far less fruitful and alive. It also seems to contradict what Christ called us to, "I have come that they may have life, and have it to the full" (John 10:10).

How we see our bodies sheds light on our self-concept: Are we unattractive and insignificant or free and fully alive? To move through and accept that which limits us can be liberating; it can increase our ability to love and be loved.

How Hormones Affect Us

Let me tell a story from my marriage to illustrate an issue that I would guess all couples have had to deal with at some point: female hormones. As we know, our hormones are not stable, but fluctuate within each month, and within a woman's lifetime go through even more dramatic changes. And whether we would like to admit it or not, hormonal changes do affect aspects of our emotional and physiological state, including our mood and personality. Women experience their own roller-coaster ride during each cycle, and men are along for the ride whether they meant to be on board or not.

My husband and I have struggled with infertility for a number of years. As part of the medical protocol, I have taken estrogen-inducing hormones at several points in the past six years. This particular event took place four years ago; it feels like it was yesterday. I was on a fertility drug that, I have since found out, fools your body into thinking you aren't producing estrogen and throws you into menopause for the cycle.

My husband had agreed to pick up groceries for dinner that evening. When he arrived home and I saw the bag he was carrying, I knew something was wrong: He had gone to the wrong store. I had in mind that he would go to another, less expensive store, and for some reason, at this moment, his choice really bothered me. However, besides indulging myself with a slightly unsupportive comment, "I didn't think you were going to Safeway," I resigned myself to take the chicken out of the bag and make dinner. It was then that our conflict began.

I pulled out not boneless chicken breasts but chicken still on the bone. I turned to him and said: "What is this? I told you chicken breasts."

"Those are chicken breasts," he replied.

In my shame at not knowing how to cook boned chicken, I snapped, "But they have bones in them; this is chicken on the bone. You must not love me. Have I ever in the five years of our marriage cooked you chicken on the bone?"

There was a painful pause. "I don't know." If only he had stopped there, but he did not. He said the worst words he could have at that particular moment: "My mom used to cook them all the time."

I do not know what the look on my face was, but the message it communicated was loud and clear. My husband said, with repressed anger, "I am going to the bathroom, and then I will take the chicken back to the store and get you what you wanted."

At that point, I burst into tears. I told him that I did not know how to cook chicken on the bone, but I would figure something out, and he absolutely could not return them to the store. You can imagine his frustration and confusion. We did not discuss the incident again that evening.

A week later I remembered the scene in the kitchen over "chicken on the bone" while I was speaking with the infertility nurse at the end of that cycle (needless to say, I was not pregnant that month). I told her, "I don't think I can do this again. I yelled at my husband for chicken on the bone." I had no idea if she knew what I was talking about, but her tone shifted and she became very nurturing: "Dear, you need to remember that your personality and moods are altered by the drugs. Those things happen." I appreciated her kindness but did not have the mental or emotional strength to try again the next month.

What I had wanted from my husband were good things: to be known (even in my cooking habits) and to be appreciated and cared for in a difficult time of medical meddling. However, it was not clear to him or myself what I needed.

For several years, I was ashamed and embarrassed about this incident. It was not until I told a friend that I finally experienced release from the shame of being a "woman with hormones." I realize now that I needed to exercise patience not only with my spouse at that time but also with myself. My heart now more closely resembles the nurse's regarding my body in transition.

After apologizing to my husband for blaming him for my condition, my challenge was to accept my situation, forgive myself, and grant myself the space to be just where my body needed to be. How often I push myself through tiredness, sadness, or anger to be what I think others need me to be. Those choices take their toll on my physical and spiritual health. When I do not listen to and care for my body, honoring it as the dwelling place of the Holy Spirit (1 Cor. 6:19), it is hard for me to pray and rest in God's presence. Our bodies and our spiritual state are closely knit.

Biblical Witness

The Bent Woman (Luke 13:10–17)

As Luke tells the story, a bent woman enters a synagogue where people have gathered to hear Jesus teach. She has been crippled, unable to stand straight, for eighteen long years. She saw life from ground level and would rarely have seen people's faces or expressions. Perhaps that spared her their inevitable disgust at her deformed shape. She would have noticed things others might not have, such as the roughness of the ground, pools of rainwater, small wild-flowers, and children at play, but she would have missed much as well. She would have had trouble embracing or being embraced; chances are that many avoided physical contact with her. Likely she couldn't conceive, her bent form not free to grow or nurture life inside her. Bent, she was vulnerable, in a humbled position. Although seeing him would have been difficult from her vantage point, she could hear Jesus speak.

The scene changes quickly as Jesus sees her, calls her forward, and says to her, "Woman, you are set free from your infirmity" (v. 12). He placed his hands on her and she immediately straightened up and praised God. He took a risk. Since it was the Sabbath, surely he knew the synagogue ruler would rebuke him, but his compassion for the bent woman superceded law-keeping and his own protection.

She had been bent over "by a spirit" (v. 11). As I read that text, I wonder what spirits have bent me over in life? What do I need to be set free from? How has my body (and/or spirit) been crushed and disfigured?

Jesus stopped teaching to call her over and heal her: His actions were his lesson lived. Jesus had compassion on her and desired her release. He knew the length of her bondage. It is unclear from the text how much this woman trusted that Jesus would heal her. We do know she trusted him enough to walk over in front of a crowd and let him put his hands on her. But she must have had hope—she did not believe that God had given up on her, or else why had she come this day to hear Jesus?

After he spoke words of healing, he put his hands on her. We might imagine that Jesus' touch was warm. Did it hurt to have a twisted spine of eighteen years straighten? The hands of the healer may have been the first in a long time to touch her tenderly. His touch communicated physical wholeness and also restoration to the fellowship of "upright people." Others may have treated her with newfound respect since she had been chosen to receive Jesus' ministry.

What of the places in us that are "bent," awaiting the healer's touch? Can we come to terms with our own bentness and offer it to God for him to heal in whatever way he sees fit? Are there ways God has used our physical suffering to communicate something of his love, tender care, compassion, and desire for our wholeness? Our bodies can guide us to greater faith and trust when they are places of physical healing or spiritual restoration.

Study Questions

How do I feel about my body? Do I accept it or do I see it as something I fight against or try to beat into submission?

How do I bring my faith and sexuality together? What is it like to consider those two words in the same sentence?

How do I celebrate life?

With which aspects of my body do I need to make peace?

How am I a "bent" woman?

8

Women Who Inspire Us

One of the benefits of remembering our stories and allowing them to speak is that we may discover a person we had forgotten. Many healing women have gone before us and can help us set a course for our future. Perhaps you were fortunate enough to have such a woman in your immediate family. Or a teacher, neighbor, favorite aunt, Sunday school leader, youth leader, or friend's mother may have inspired you. Even a character in fiction or in a film can capture the imagination of a girl and help her dream toward who she is becoming as a woman. As I recall my own journey, I am aware of numerous female faces that have helped give shape to my own. Some of these were women I had met; others were women I read about or observed in a museum. In different ways, each has offered me direction, inspiration, and visions of healing.

Words of Hope

A folk singer named Dar Williams tells a wonderful tale of friendship and deliverance in the song, "You're Aging Well."[1] She put words to a girl's interaction with an older, wiser woman. She describes how the young girl's confusion over what demands life would make of her, particularly in terms of her weight, led her to attempt suicide. It was in this place that an older woman came along and rescued her. This wise, older woman had much to offer because she had overcome difficult experiences in her own life. She had been hardened by circumstances until the day her heart changed. At one point, she realized that telling her story could be powerful: "The story you'll tell. And no sooner than spoken, a spell had been broken." All of a sudden, things she had tried to deny turned into beautiful instruments of sound, which were "music around her" as she moved through life.

It was from this place of healing that the wise woman was able to see the young girl's plight and offer her "the language that keeps me alive." Those words were, "I'm so glad you finally made it here. With the things you know now, that only time could tell. Looking back, seeing far, landing right where we are, and you're aging well, aren't we aging well."[2]

An older woman who has known healing of her own story and past can impart hope to those who come after her. In the song, when the older woman recognized that her story was worth telling, her past was transformed into something of magnificent beauty and sound. It was this music that drew others to her and then brought them strength. To have a woman you respect look at you in the midst of your struggle (perhaps even shame at trying to quit) and say, "You're aging well"—those are holy, healing words.

The painful parts of our stories equip us to be beautiful bearers of healing for others. Will you stop running long enough to let them bless you?

Grammy Alice—My Inspiration

One woman who has had a profound influence on my life is my grandmother, whom we called Grammy Alice. She died when I was nine years old. Although I only knew her in my childhood, my life continues to bear her imprint. I still miss her.

As a child, I remember her delicious, warm chocolate chip cookies. She would bake them for us at least once during our weeklong visits to her home in South Carolina. The long drive from Connecticut to Myrtle Beach likely taxed my parents' patience, and I was stuck in the backseat for many hours with my energetic younger brother, but it was all worth it for the moment of arrival in her driveway. Immediately, I was intoxicated by the smell of sweet pine needles and the salt air from the ocean.

Grammy warmed me by her generous love. She and I had special hobbies that we shared, just between the two of us. We collected large, heavy books about dollhouses and miniatures. These were "our" books, and Grammy pulled them out each time I came to visit. We would spend what felt like hours pouring through the shiny pages of pictures, identifying the tiny objects, and discussing how these dainty items were made. I also remember going on long walks with her on the beach, among the sand dunes, collecting shells.

One distinct impression I have of Grammy is her hand—tanned, freckled, with opal and ruby diamond rings on her fingers. I remember studying and holding that hand, and feeling such love for this woman who showered me with boundless affection. For some reason, my mental image of her hand is most vividly associated with a particular drive in her light blue Buick with white, leather interior. As she drove, she rested her hand calmly on the armrest beside her. From where I sat tucked in the backseat it was the part of her I could see most clearly. She and my mom were discussing my grandfather's health. He had just survived his third stroke, and Mom and Grammy were deciding how best to care for him once he was released from the hospital. Grammy and BaBill were supposed to move in the coming weeks. Grammy was talking about getting the rest of the boxes packed, preparing the house to sell, and moving to Florida. The mood in the car was serious, but I recall feeling joy that I was with these two women I loved. Little did I know this would be the last time I would see Grammy; within a week of our departure she died from a massive coronary.

Grammy Alice was a woman of substance and strength. After struggling for nine years to conceive her second child (my mom), her first husband left her with a two-month-old and a ten-year-old. In those days, divorce was particularly shameful, but she did not waste any time on self-pity. She took the commuter train into Manhattan and pursued a successful career as an editor at Doubleday. Alice had been an exceptional student, having skipped several grades throughout school, so although she had no formal training or experience in editing, Doubleday saw that "something" in her that quietly proclaimed, "I can do whatever I set my mind to."

Alice struggled to be a good single mom to her two daughters. They all lived with her parents, who helped raise the girls; they walked the girls to school since Alice had to get up early to catch the train to the city. It was on this train that, eight years later, she met her future husband, known as BaBill to his grandchildren.

Alice worked hard, had spunk and energy, and was loved by all who knew her as a kind, strong woman. She wore vibrant colors and zany glasses, and she gave the most exciting and unusual gifts. All her relatives and friends enjoyed the power of her presence.

Grammy never lost her love for books. I remember her in her retirement years, reading volume after volume as she sat in a white chaise lounge in her room—still learning, growing, discovering. I now have that chaise. I remember her well as I sit in it.

When I consider my life, the choices I have made, the issues that have captured my imagination, I realize that Grammy Alice is very much a part of me. From her I gained my love of books, work, and learning. I appreciate the tenacity it took for her to live so robustly, despite having been left with so much responsibility and so little space to grieve her losses. I know I have a legacy to live up to and to honor.[3]

Art as Invitation

Standing before the *Pietá* in St. Peter's Basilica in Vatican City, I was silenced. Knowing that I could not lean back on the great marble pillars, lest the Vatican police come and correct me in a less than gentle tone, I tried to balance on my tourist-tired legs and consider this impressive work of art. Seated before me was a powerfully expressive statue of Mary holding her crucified son on her lap. Her face is that of a young girl, ageless; she looks serene yet sad. Her downcast eyes are fixed on her son, but they are filled with an expression of love and peace. The great folds of her robe undergird her son's body, as once swaddling clothes had surrounded him. Her arms are open wide to receive her son, with one hand held out to heaven in open supplication. Her lap looks proportionate to her body but is wide enough to comfortably hold her limp son's body.

I pondered the width of this young woman's lap that could hold not only the life-size body of a grown man, but that also could contain the sorrow of this scene with a serenity that promises, "This is not the end of the story." I wondered what Michelangelo was thinking as he chiseled away at this great piece of marble. Did he hope to capture the timelessness of Mary's beauty and youth? Did he want to honor the sacredness of her countenance by avoiding anguished looks of grief and rage over the death of a mother's child? The paradox of magnificent beauty juxtaposed with a scene of lament allured me. Standing amidst the throng of pilgrims from the far reaches of the globe, I stared, unashamedly transfixed by the scene before me.

I never quite understood Mary. I was raised Protestant, and since I knew my Catholic friends prayed to her, I thought I needed to distance myself from her for fear of committing a sin against God. As I have grown older and stood before other such Marian works, I have become aware of the Catholic understanding that God's image is reflected in both males and females. There is something in their reverence toward this humble woman that reminds me of the feminine nature of the Godhead. Is this something Protestants have lost?

It may be time for Protestants to rediscover the value of this "God-carrier" and explore what we can learn from her as we come to know the mysterious God that we serve. Certainly, her words in the Magnificat draw our focus to God and prompt us to remember his works of love and faithfulness. Perhaps her great lap is wide enough not only to contain the pain and suffering of a fallen world but also to remind us of a love so great that God would sacrifice his only begotten Son on our behalf. No greater love than this could come from any parent.[4]

Theology as Spiritual Food

My favorite theologian is a woman who intrigues me by the breadth of her knowledge and her humble faith. Simone Weil, whom I mentioned in chapter 5, lived in the first half of the twentieth century and combined science, math, politics, history, and philosophy to talk powerfully about God and faith. She has been described as one of the greatest spiritual thinkers of our century. Her life is full of contrasts and intrigue. She defies categorization. She offered powerful insights on the place of suffering in the life of the Christian. For her, suffering was the seedbed for true worship. As I wrestle with my clients in their places of loss, I find words of guidance and inspiration from Weil.

Her humility is manifest in the way she came to faith in Jesus. She found herself in a little Portuguese village for the festival of their patron saint. She saw a procession of fishermen carrying candles. "There the conviction was suddenly borne in upon me that Christianity is preeminently the religion of slaves, that slaves cannot help belonging to it, and I among others."[5] She also spent two days praying at the chapel of Assisi, where "something stronger than I was compelled me for the first time in my life to go down on my knees."[6] Later, at a liturgical service, suffering from piercing headaches, she felt she was,

> able to rise above this wretched flesh, to leave it to suffer by itself, heaped up in a corner, and to find a pure and perfect joy in the unimaginable beauty of the chanting and the words. This experience enabled me by analogy to get a better understanding of the possibility of loving divine love in the midst of affliction. It goes without saying that in the course of these services the thought of the Passion of Christ entered into my being once and for all.[7]

Through his own despair, Christ could identify with even the most abject sufferer. This compassion is something Simone Weil prized. She wanted to share Christ's ability to understand and reach down into the heart of those who hurt. Weil did not just write about human suffering, but she sought out the poor, mistreated, war torn people of Europe. Her writing and story are compelling.

Weil died when she was thirty-four. While in England during World War II, she was diagnosed with tuberculosis. She deprived herself, refusing to eat more than the rations her compatriots received in France. She wanted to show her solidarity with those in occupied France. Because of her illness, this rationing was a form of starvation; the newspapers claimed it was suicide. She died relatively unknown. Possibly one of the greatest minds of this century, she was buried in a peasant's grave, in a foreign land, with few mourners. She was a woman who did not seek her own fame but sought anonymity and solidarity with the suffering, on behalf of the gospel—I consider her a wonderful mentor even though I have only met her in print.

Spirituality as Conviction

A modern nun, Macrina Wiederkehr, describes finding the holy in the ordinary in her book, *A Tree Full of Angels*. She offers powerful pointers to the gospel in our lives in ways that provoke a sense of reverence and humility in her readers. She has been a monastic for forty years, one of the sisters of St. Scholastica, a Benedictine monastery in Fort Smith, Arkansas. Her writing captures the heart's desire to find and follow Jesus.

One of her lines has powerful counseling implications, "I understand now that it can be a good prayer to weep over the person you've refused to become."[8] Macrina acknowledges that we have a holy privilege as God's children to live up to a grand calling, but we often deny it by holding ourselves back and not becoming all that God would have for us. She invites her readers to have more—more life, hope, and faith. She writes about spirituality in a woman's voice.

Sister Macrina's understanding of God goes beyond doctrinal words: Her understanding is experiential. Part of her ministry is to help others appreciate that their own experience of life and faith is valuable. She calls others to join the quest for the "holy in the ordinary." I have come away from her books touched, impacted, and challenged to open my heart more fully to the love of God evident all around, in, and through us. In her writing, I am reminded to "have eyes to see and ears to hear" the gospel in all of my circumstances.

From family to art, theology to music, the preceding stories express a few of the places God has found me through the lives and love of other women in my life. From these voices, and others, I have learned something about being a healing woman. I invite you to take your own journey: Rediscover the faces of the women who have modeled strength, compassion, and wisdom to you. Notice what they taught you of God and how they shaped your budding faith. Perhaps the ways they intrigued you and invited you to life are already features of who you have become. Even their gestures, favorite words, crusades, and interests could be part of you. Certainly, their faces have helped shape your self-image. Acknowledging your own face allows you to stand in God's presence and taste his delight in you.

Biblical Witness

Mary, the Mother of Jesus (Luke 1:26–38)

The list of women who inspire us would not be complete without reflecting on a young woman's assent to being used by God for bringing his greatest gift to the world. When I was young, I often wondered if I was growing into womanhood as Mary did. I was not sure I would be able to believe that something implausible and threatening to my reputation might inspire words like "May it be to me as you have said." I doubted I had what it took. I tried to imagine what Mary might have reported after an angel showed up with some surprising news.

"I definitely felt fear. Having an angel appear in my little town of Nazareth is not a daily occurrence. And it never happens to teenage girls, at least not any I know. What do I do with what I have seen?

"The angel frightened me. But his words spoke to the troubled places of my heart. He said, 'Do not be afraid, Mary, you have found favor with God.' How kind of him to reassure me. I suppose he wanted me to be calm enough to hear the other incredible news he had to bring. God has found favor with me. I wonder why? What great things have I accomplished in my short life? I am merely trying to learn how to take on the roles expected of me when I become a wife and mother. I did not think I was 'exceptional' in the eyes of the great God of Abraham, Isaac, and Jacob.

"Not only am I chosen, which seems too great to comprehend, but I am to bear a child for God. I am stunned by that revelation. I asked the angel, 'How will this be since I am a virgin?' Clearly, the mechanics of all this don't make sense. But the angel told me God's Spirit will overshadow me. That makes me think that a giant bird will come down and hover over me with its strong wings. I will be comforted in its shade. I guess I need to trust that if God wants this to happen, it will, according to his design. After all, he provided the ram for Abraham so he did not have to sacrifice his son; he parted the Red Sea for my people as they fled their Egyptian masters. He is capable of great deeds.

"This pregnancy will be viewed as ill-timed by the people in my village, my parents, and particularly my fiancé. I wonder if people will believe me or understand. Does God know how hard this might be for me? Maybe because of my youth, I am ready to trust this messenger of God both that I have been chosen and that I will bear a child out of wedlock.

"After the angel said to me, 'Nothing is impossible with God,' I realized that all I could do was trust him, and that was what my heart most deeply longed to do. If he could work out the impossible, surely he would guide me in the details. When the angel left, I knew I had been entrusted with a costly calling. I would spend the rest of my life realizing the significance of what that moment of saying 'yes' to God would mean for me and for the world."

Study Questions

Which women in my life have offered me hope?

Who has taught me how to be a woman?

Where do I go for inspiration on living?

Have there been works of art that have moved me? What books on God and faith have changed me?

9

Expectancy

In February of 1996, I wrote these words in a journal, "I would not be in counseling unless I believed people are more enjoyable and attractive than they want me to believe that they are." Those words still ring true. Each time someone walks into my office, I am convinced that behind their defenses and the ways they try to hide their irrevocable image of God, each person is delightful and worth getting to know. Despite their dress, their appearance, their seeming indifference at sitting across from me, I believe there is more, much more, to each person than meets the eye.

Loretta—A Challenging Case

It had not been an easy life for the woman in midlife who sat across from me, facing the door. Every so often she eyed her exit with a sense of relish. I wondered just which week she would get up during our session and not return. We had worked together for several months, and I admit that I felt counselor-defeat before a hard case—finding the jewel in the haystack with her would not come without cost.

Loretta had every reason to distrust me. She had seen countless other counselors, been misdiagnosed, prescribed ineffectual medications, and had even spent several seasons in psychiatric care. She had a deep distrust not only for medical types but even for anyone in a position of authority. I knew we would have an uphill battle from the moment she walked into my office.

Loretta's appearance was notably unkempt. Her clothes looked worn and unclean. They hung about her slumped shoulders like a pile of discolored rags. Her lined face showed the hardness of the path she had traveled and the many injustices she had endured. She often scowled with displeasure, creasing two deep ridges in her forehead.

In moments of frustration, I wondered why I had agreed to see her. Did I want to prove to myself that I could win over the most unlovable people and offer healing? I chastised myself for my professional arrogance. Any thoughts of saving this woman from herself were far from my mind on the particular Friday that Loretta surprised me.

We had just met with one of the numerous internal walls she put up when faced with any conversation that had a fighting chance of leading somewhere constructive (at least in my humble therapeutic opinion). I sat back, prepared to receive one of her scathing remarks about my intrusive nature and why therapists have nothing to say to her. She paused, sensing my frustration, and said, "I have really been a pain, haven't I?" I looked at her, stunned. She was offering a peace pipe. Instead of continuing to test me, keeping her guard up, and mocking my inabilities to reach her, she finally owned that she was a difficult person. Her tone was kinder than usual, even inviting.

Thoughts swirled through my mind and were likely evident on my face. Why today? What had changed between us that now it was safe to invite me into her life and heart? Perhaps she was afraid that I was getting ready to refer her to someone else "who might be able to help you better than I can." Whatever the reason, she sat across from me with an impish grin on her face, waiting for me to respond.

I knew we had made a turn, and although counseling would still be a struggle, we had moved into another place, one in which she invited me to be with her. Given her story, I knew the invitation was an honor. I responded with words that captured my surprise and delight, "Loretta, I am so glad to meet you. It's good to finally make your acquaintance."

Anticipation

I approach the people with whom I work with anticipation; I am eager to find out what makes them tick, how they find hope in the midst of losses, and how they face each day with the weight of the burdens they carry. As we journey together, I know that times of joy and celebration in their progress may be followed by a crushing sense of self-defeat and hopelessness. I look forward with them to the day they "graduate" from counseling, both of us knowing they have the tools, the faith, and the resources to continue the battle without me. Before each final meeting I anticipate both the joyful remembrances together as well as my grief at losing the story and the person that has become a part of my story in the past weeks, months, or years.

117

My clients and students have taught me much over the years about the importance of having hope. Without hope, we have no energy to get out of bed. Hope says there is a future worth working, living, and striving for and discovering. Hope is courage for the cares of today. Hope also does not come easy.

Hope as a concept can seem disconnected from where we live, but it is embodied in our ability to choose. When we get out of bed, hit the alarm, and get ready for work, we are choosing our lives.[1] If we choose life today, then we have the power to choose differently tomorrow. Hope is a choice—not a feeling.

For many people, life does not feel like a choice. They feel driven by their schedule, by their need to meet others' needs, fulfill a quota, pay the bills/rent/loans, do as well as the next person. "Where are my choices?" they may ask. They argue themselves out of hope: "If I can escape seeing other options in the way of doing things, then I am not responsible to change or do better than merely survive and demand that others appreciate the depths of my struggle. I might prefer being pitied to being challenged to live better." But they may recognize that there is more to life than that. "Good parts of my heart know that I am made for more than what I settle for. I want to change and I don't." This is the heart of the term *ambivalence:* It gums up the works of daily functioning.

If I want to change yet also do not want to change, then I am stuck, unable to move. For some, that means staying trapped in a pit of depression. One client could talk about his hope for his friends and family, but he had no sense of hope for himself. He felt adrift in the sea of life without any moorings to steady himself. He expressed this to me as, "I don't trust my judgment. What is my goal, and how do I situate my life around it?" I invited him, "in the future, I hope you will hope for yourself as much as you are willing to do so for others in your life." His indecision about his life and his unwillingness to dream kept him safe from hope's demands.

We often fear hope. After all, hope ignites our passions, requires our transformation, and invites us to dream wild dreams and to believe in an unseen God. Any one of these is risky and reminds us of our vulnerability. Hope invites us to a place where we are not in control of the outcome. Is it really wise to open that door to possibility and mystery?

When I was in graduate school, trying to sort through my life, my issues, and a sense of calling, these words came to me:

Desire Awakening

I cringe
the painful cords of desire rip free from her safe moorings
the dark night beckons
the heavy sails fill
heavy stillness expectant with hope and terror shrouds
   the bow
Too late to turn back
Too soon to know where the tidewater will take us
is there a destination or is the journey an unending tale
no more ports, docks, locks,
only open seas
whose depths are too deep to plumb
vast, wide,
abounding in mystery, promise, and danger.

What was it I was afraid to see in others and myself? To hope is to realize that I am not in control. It requires faith and the courage to acknowledge that I have needs.

Being Needy People

What is neediness? The world's definition would be one of clinginess, desperation, grasping for a lifeline—a needy person is one who will suck you down into their black hole or vortex. The poet John Ciardi addressed these issues in a poem called "Aunt Mary." He writes, "Now what shall I pray for gluttonous Aunt Mary who loved us till we screamed? Even poor mother had more of Aunt Mary's love than she could live with, but had to live with it."[2] Sometimes needy love can be crushing and confining. But this is not a biblical perspective on being needy.

In Isaiah 55:1–3a, we see a picture of God as one who affirms that we thirst and hunger. He calls our desire good because it draws us to his outstretched arms. Without the need we might not hear his promise of provision or his care.

> "Come, all you who are thirsty, come to the waters;
> and you who have no money,
>   come, buy and eat!
> Come, buy wine and milk
>   without money and without cost.
> Why spend money on what is not bread,
>   and your labor on what does not satisfy?
> Listen, listen to me, and eat what is good,
>   and your soul will delight in the richest of fare.
> Give ear and come to me;
>   hear me, that your soul may live."

We are called to seek true satisfaction, the quenching of all for which our deepest desires cry. We are called to delight in God, to delight that what he offers will fill and nourish the sacred places of our souls. Are we promised immediate gratification in response to our requests? Or is there an eschatological aspect to his filling? Just as we see in a glass dimly on this side of heaven, our need cannot be fully met or we would not recognize that we do not yet apprehend all that is God. We, on earth, can taste crumbs and be reminded of what we have always hoped: that in heaven there will be complete fulfillment, a rich spread set for hearts that will remain hungry until the end of our days.

In *The Message,* Eugene Peterson paraphrases Luke's presentation of the Beatitudes this way:

> "You're blessed when you've lost it all.
> God's kingdom is there for the finding.
>
> You're blessed when you're ravenously hungry.
> Then you're ready for the Messianic meal.
>
> You're blessed when the tears flow freely.
> Joy comes with the morning."
>
> Luke 6:20–21

In the Beatitudes, Christ contrasts the poor with the rich and self-reliant. To the poor, he says that theirs is the kingdom now, not in the future. Luke emphasizes need—those who need will be satisfied. In Matthew's version, we see that these words were meant to go deeper than material poverty or physical hunger. Matthew describes a poverty of spirit and hunger for righteousness.

To hope is to be needy and, furthermore, to admit our need. You and I are much more in tune with our physical needs than our spiritual ones, yet God captures our fleshly imaginations by promising to be the bread of life and an unending supply of living waters. A story attributed to Mother Teresa describes what happens when you offer a starving child a piece of bread. A child that is starving to death has a distended belly and feels bloated, even full, because its hunger pains have disappeared. To offer that child a piece of bread is incredibly cruel, because its hunger pains will return, and its stomach will begin to growl ferociously. Yet without that bread the child will die. Just as the child needs to feel its hunger to prompt it to eat, without our own sense of spiritual hunger, we are unaware of how desperately we need God, and there is no room for him to work in us. We need to remember that he is the one in whom we live and move and have our being.

What does it mean to believe that God takes our suffering and redeems it? Look at those to whom Jesus ministered. Jesus reached out to the foot-washing prostitute, the thirsty Samaritan, the bleeding woman, the leprous man, and the hungry multitude; he offered them healing, food, life, forgiveness, and soul-quenching satisfaction.

Christ himself was needy and hungry as he journeyed for forty days in the wilderness. Satan offered him three temptations. He tempted Christ with what we consider important for human needs: food, power, glory. Christ refused, believing there was something higher. He who could have had his needs met refused to announce his significance through spiritual power, kingly rule, and physical nourishment. He chose isolation over community. He refused all of what we might define as necessary and chose to remain needy.

Note that Satan spoke to Christ when he was needy. Using people's need against them is a powerful tool in Satan's arsenal. It wasn't until after Jesus prevailed over Satan that God appears on the pages of Scripture, through the angels, to minister to Christ. We wonder, was God silent during Jesus' desert days? Will he at times be silent through ours as well? Are we willing to wait for the angels, or will we give in to temptation? In his fasting, solitude, and struggle, Jesus exemplified perfect submission to his Father's will despite experiencing great human need. His physical neediness allowed him to taste more deeply the substance of his Father.

How does God respond to our need? There are moments when God brilliantly intervenes. I have had my own Jordan River experience. I was out of college, having spent almost a year as a personnel consultant in data processing placement outside New York City. That was the hardest job I have ever had. Although there are many reputable recruiting firms, I, unfortunately, did not end up at one. In this job, I was expected to be pushy, angry, and demanding. Everything inside me recoiled at this. The job was straight commission; in a year, I saw twelve colleagues hired, only to see them quit. It was neither an easy job nor a friendly work environment. In disgust, I called my job "professional prostitution."

Needless to say, when my minister called and invited me to join a trip to the Holy Land that was leaving in two weeks, I celebrated. I saw the trip as God's gift of freedom. I went to work the next morning and tried to give my two-week notice. I informed them I was most likely going to go to seminary in the fall. After they recovered from their amazement, they insisted I return after my trip and finish working the summer. I think I may have been the first head-hunter they had known for whom the job drove them into the arms of seminary.

I went to the Holy Land feeling gifted with two weeks of freedom—freedom to walk in Jesus' steps and to experience the terrain and culture of the Bible's homeland. It was incredible. My most powerful memory is that of being immersed in the Jordan River. I waited in a line of fellow pilgrims to be prayed over and dipped down into the waters. My prayer request to the minister was that I would truly turn over all that I am and will be to the God who made me. The hurting, needy, raw place in my heart that had struggled with disbelief all year at the madness that my life had become surrendered in that river. I wanted more than anything to give all my need, all my substance, all my lack to him. Most of all, I ached for a taste of God himself.

As the minister set me down into the water and then raised me back up, I felt an overwhelming tear inside. Something in me was broken, torn asunder, laid bare. I wept great, heaving tears, which I had never done before, and, even more amazingly, I did so in public. I wept as the saints sang their hymns and praise songs reverently on the banks of the Jordan. I wept at the renewed longing in me for God and at his incredible gift of himself to me in that river. It seemed that God offered me a fraction of a taste of how much he loves me, and had he given me any greater sense of that reality, I would have died from the intensity of it. As it was, I felt filled to the point of bursting. Yes, "Blessed are those who hunger and thirst for righteousness, for they will be filled" (Matt. 5:6).

Yet there are plenty of days that are not Jordan River experiences. There are days of silence when I am left yearning for something I do not have. Not every need is filled, taken care of, or resolved. We live in a dangerous world where to want is lunacy and to wait is cowardly. It is in our dark days, however, that faith can take root and we have the opportunity to trust in the unseen God. What sustains us is our memory of times when we were more aware of his presence than we are today. Only that can quiet our raging hearts.

Are you willing to stay alive and groan with creation while you await the day of redemption (see Rom. 8:22)? Or will you choose to walk away from God and your own neediness to die to true living? To be alive is to need, to grieve, to feel, to laugh, to love. Despite the danger of living in a world that will wound us, there is something about the gospel our stories will tell if we are willing to ache and to wait on a God who has done the same for us.

As Macrina Wiederkehr put it:

> God, you cannot hide from me. You cannot scare me with your face of absence. I scare myself with this hunger for your presence. I would break all rules to possess you. To be nourished by you, I would go to every table in the world. I would leave no stone unturned to find you lest when I turn it over it be changed to bread. I come look-

ing for bread, but if you're saving it for your children don't worry. I'll gather up the crumbs if you insist, I'll make a meal on leftovers and rejoice that I have been so blessed. O Most Powerful One, I feel so powerless, so little and so poor, so vulnerable, so terribly wide open, so seen. It hurts to be so hungry, so dependent on your bits of grace.[3]

Will you risk admitting your hunger pains? Invite God and others to minister to your needy soul. Go and want. Go and be filled. Go and ask, seek, and knock. God longs to feed you. Even more he longs to welcome you home with a loving embrace that will overwhelm you with fullness.

Biblical Witness

Knowing My Need—Hannah (1 Samuel 1–2:10)

Am I willing to be mocked at the very point of my deepest pain? That is the question that I, Hannah, wife of Elkanah, have to face day in and day out. If it was not enough that my spouse's other wife, Peninnah, flaunts her fertility and misses no occasion to humiliate my empty womb, now the local rabbi thinks I have come to prayer drunk. Where is there safety from the ache in my heart? Will you ever hear my cry, great Jehovah? Where is your justice?

My story so often gets told: Because I believed in God, he heard my cry and brought me my son. However, those telling my story usually rush through my years of torment, waiting, despairing, desiring, begging Elkanah for a child. I tried all the old wives' tales to conceive; in the end, that day in the temple, I was ready to quit. Nothing else had worked. Nor did I have any hope left that it would or could. I was ready to invite God to take me and relieve me of the great emptiness in my heart and body. I was created by him for womanhood, given by him to a faithful man, and then forgotten, left on the ash heap of life, useless without children to preserve me. I was barren, desolate, broken by the weight of my need.

Yet I had not let go of hope entirely. If I had, I would not have been praying in the temple that day. A war raged in my chest about giving up or pressing on, about continuing to want or trying to kill desire. I had tried to not want, to not care, to not need a child, but I did not win that battle. I am beginning to see that this battle is not my own. I am trying to kill something in me that God won't allow me to succeed in shutting down. It must be far too important to him that I have a place of need. Maybe that place is just where he can be found.

I may be slowed down by defeat, weighty with want, and longing for his reign and justice, but I *am* now open to need and want God. Had I been given a full womb, with lots of offspring, perhaps I would never have been in this place. A misunderstood woman praying passionately to the God who lets "justice roll on like a river" (Amos 5:24a)—that may be just what God intended. I must wait, I must want, and I must live expectantly. Then, when he finally acts and answers—my song will be sweet enough to record for generations and generations to come.

Study Questions

Who are the challenging people in my life? How do I handle them?

What am I willing to let myself hope for and anticipate?

Do I see myself as a "needy" person? How do I feel about that word? Do I risk communicating my needs to others or to God?

What place in my life is without hope today? (Write a letter to God just to tell him how you feel about this without rushing to a conclusion. Let the note be more of a lament. Try picking up the letter a few days later and seeing what more you can add to your words. Note if your heart is moving toward God on this issue even if the situation is no clearer.)

10

The Blessing of Limitation

We are finite beings. We have limits. There is something about becoming aware of boundaries to our capabilities that can help us live with what we have in the moment more alive. We all know people who refuse to accept that they do not have enough talent, money, beauty, smarts, or time. The "if only's" of existence ensnare and keep us from being present in the life, relationships, and opportunities we do have.

Karen Horney, an early pioneer in the field of psychology, believed we must all accept the "ordinariness of one's real self."[1] I have found these simple yet profound words to be true. In my own life, it is my superhuman thinking and attempts at living that get me into trouble: I want to come up with a great plan for solving problems for people, marriages, organizations—even world peace. Perhaps if only I try a little harder or work a little more frenetically, I can, through sheer physical effort alone, bring about change. Notice that this self-centered approach to life is void of others and God. Given that I do not have infinite abilities or stamina, the triumph goes unattained. I am left remembering the words of Horney and my need to accept my "ordinariness." I need to be aware of what God has invited me to tend today and leave the rest (even the work of tending) up to him. I am *a worker* in the vineyard, not the workers, owner, vines, grapes, tools, and seasons. I often need a perspective adjustment.

Life Has Limits

Sometimes a single incident changes us forever. It permanently alters our perception. The following is one such incident in my life. After witnessing this event, I turned to journaling as a way of coming to terms with the powerful reality of what transpired: "Tonight, on this Amtrak car a man crossed the divide and went to stand before his Creator. Was he an elder in his church? Did he have children and family? What was his profession?"

Rescue personnel carried by my seat a heavyset man with a scar running down his exposed chest. Big brown shoes passed me first, then his pants, loosened and hanging open around his hips. The paramedics wedged their hands around his shoulders through the narrow aisle. After twenty-five minutes of CPR the rescue team removed the victim from the train, carrying him out to a mat on the platform where they put electric shocks on his chest. I will never forget the sight of that broad, exposed stomach and the brown shoes—they were worn on the soles, never to be worn again. I felt as if I was peering into an open casket as it was pushed into a hearse. Other passengers had followed the paramedics, carrying this man's earthly possessions: a red silk tie, a walkman, a briefcase, and a coat. But he could not take them with him; he had already gone ahead. The train continued its grinding speed through the dispassionate suburbs.

The people whose curiosity had led them onto our car to watch that man die trickled back to their seats. The policewoman standing next to me exited with the rescue team. The two nurses who had come in and taken charge in the crisis returned to their car. The conductor resumed his post and tried to figure out how to get us back on schedule and onto the correct track.

The only one who seemed affected by what had transpired here was the young paramedic with a half-shaved head of hair, a fellow passenger. I had first seen him when I ran back two cars yelling, "Is there a doctor on the train?" He stood and said, "I am a paramedic." We ran back to my car together. He was the one who put his lips on this man's mouth and breathed into his lungs, trying to push all his life into helping this other man hang on to his own. An unsung hero. After twenty-five minutes of hard work, when the rescue squad and ambulance took over, removing the victim from the scene, the paramedic stood in the aisle, wiping the sweat and tears from his face. His eyes were wet and swollen. He looked at me, put both hands on my shoulders, and said, "Are you okay?" I guess I looked a little pale and shaky as I sipped water. I said, "I am fine." He said, "Where are my nurses? I want to see those nurses who helped me." I directed him, "People say they are two cars ahead." He paused, trying to summon the strength to continue up the train. I went back and filled a cup of water for him. He took it and went on. I hope he found them. Later, he came back through the car, still looking exhausted.

As the man in the seat next to me exited, I said, "We can say a prayer for our friend tonight." As other businessmen exited, they agreed to call Amtrak to complain that they do not carry oxygen on their trains for just such emergencies. They felt it could have been any of them in his shoes. Later, I wrote: "This man's life might have been spared, or was it your plan, Lord? I guess I have to leave it in your hands. Yours alone."

We live through life-changing moments. Each moment has the capacity to change us if we dare to let it do so. On that Amtrak train, I had a profound awareness of my limits and life's limits. I was left with many unanswerable questions: Could I have done more? Who will tell this man's story to his family? What of the story of the heroism of the tireless paramedic? Life's limits raise many questions that draw me to relationship with the question giver—the only One capable of responding to them.

Limits Misunderstood

What are our limits? In my office, I hear countless examples. People have confided they do not have enough money, enough knowledge, or enough time. Time is a poignant concern when the person has found out they or a loved one is ill. Some limits are imposed from without: health, economic injustice, or educational benefits. Others are imposed from within—these are far more tenacious.

There is a dark side to limits, because we can use them to justify our resistance to God working in us. One man believed he was limited in his wisdom: "If I were smart (I have never been smart—my folks were sure to tell me that from the start), I would figure out a way to stop getting in trouble, drinking too much, and winding up with a different woman every other night." Another man believed his was a great destiny, but that until God handed him the marching orders, he did not need to live with integrity and responsibility in the meantime.

One woman strongly disliked different aspects of her looks and body. She believed that if only she had more

131

beauty, the man at work would desire her more than his present girlfriend. Another woman complained that she was too old to try to be loving or open to those around her: "I have made it thus far without doing so, and frankly, I don't think it makes any sense to change now. I don't want to look at my past. What happened, happened. It is over now. No use looking backwards."

These people perceived their limitations as firm boundaries that allowed them to escape their call to be faithful people in the midst of struggle. They used limits to excuse themselves from any demands God or others placed upon them.

What does it mean to honestly accept our limitations without using them as an excuse to not try, choose, risk, or live? The answer to that question is unique to each person's situation. What might be a faithful surrender on the part of one person would be a willful disregard for God's call for another. A guiding question for those considering if their view of their own limits is accepting or excusing themselves would be, "Does this self-understanding move me toward others and God in relationship or does it allow me to run away from the struggle and joys of loving?" In a positive sense, limits offer us boundaries that can help us to avoid taking on the task of running the universe and that can help us see where we are and what we are invited to for this day. They remind us we are not our own but have been created and redeemed by God for something bigger than we can see and can manufacture.

We can come to terms with what limits us and find freedom, even find God, in our weakness. How ironic that it is the times when I have failed and had to apologize as a teacher or group leader that have impacted my students the most. God seems to strip things away so that I remember it is not I who is ultimately in control. I am reminded to love him by the words of the marriage vow, "in plenty and in want." I have many opportunities to show God I love him in the seasons and cycles my life has taken—from serving God by being a pastoral worship leader every Sunday to a part-time job in graduate school cleaning houses. From stoles and robes to toilet scrubbers, I have many opportunities to know God and be known in my weakness.

To have "roles" given and removed, even temporarily, can be purifying. It strips us of our dependence on our own value and reminds us God gives and takes away. I was serving a church after completing my master of divinity degree. My pastoral "role" made me feel significant, but it covered up a sense of personal inadequacy: "Would people want me if I were just Heather?" At times, I knew the role could become a source of worth apart from God. In God's graciousness, I believe he used me despite this fact.

Within a few years, my husband and I attended another master's program. We felt called to counseling as part of our future ministries. It was during that season that the toilet scrubber became my new work tool. From concordances, exegetical materials, and ministry journals to soaps, brushes, and window-cleaning fluid—I smile, in hindsight, at God's methods of guarding my heart. Humility was far more important than fame. I am grateful.

Following are the words from a journal seven months into my time of giving up a "role" and receiving something sacred in return (2/9/94):

> Heal the broken heart in me. How stained I feel as my addiction to being significant is exposed. I am anxious that the great God of creation can see my insides. There are places I would rather not recognize and which I confess I am unable to repair. Fear grips me as I consider that you invite me to bring those sins to the light, to your light for healing. But Lord, don't you understand that I would rather deny, pretend, and cover up these blemishes on my soul? The very task I fear is now put back on me. "Give them up." In a strange way, sins are insecurities I cling to because they are known. I have used

them to make sense of the cosmos and of myself. My head understands the dilemma, but it is hard for my hands to live out the way to God.

I know, God, I am of no use until I abandon my agenda in search of yours. I do wish to be stretched. Move me out of the place of abundance I have tried to manufacture for myself and lead me to the only place that will truly satisfy. I easily settle for less in fear that the best will require more of me than I can afford to give. Yet the streams of living water lie ahead. The path may be thorny and branches thick to traverse. The climb may be lonely and I may not make it to the summit. But to stop here, when the journey has been started and so many answers await; I know there is no choice but to proceed. My King awaits me at the journey's end. I face only what my Beloved knew I would and could in his strength. Make my feet swift and nimble. As a calf dances forth from its stall in the morning sun, make my song of praise beautiful for you, my Lord and love. "You will go out and leap like calves released from the stall" (Mal. 4:2).

Limits can free us. They can point us back to God. We are given the gift of needing him once again. We can bring God our empty cups so that he can fill them, perhaps even to overflowing.

Biblical Witness

The Widow's Mite (Luke 21:1–4)

A mite is a very small, inconsequential amount in terms of "giving that counts" for the temple coffers. Certainly the size of the gift would invite one to turn away in politeness so as not to point out its meagerness, despite the poverty of the giver. But that was not what Jesus did. As he looked up, he saw her.

He chose not only to see and speak about such an event but also to highlight it as an act of great faith and trust in God. He elevated this woman without means, rights, or social standing. She, whom others would overlook, became the heroine and the example.

This woman may have felt embarrassed as she went to place her offering in the temple's collection plate. Why offer such a low gift? God could not feed his poorest with this token of two small copper coins; it would not go far in terms of temple building projects; why even bother? The other givers that surrounded her would see what little she had to bring. Their disdain and enjoyment at their own largesse would stifle a woman left without a kinsman-redeemer. She gave out of her poverty, need, and hunger. It was all she had, and it was more than enough.

A widow's mite: It was all that she could give, and it was more than enough for God to use her and the gift itself for the work of his kingdom. It was only a mite, but it was all of a mite.

Study Questions

What are some of my limits that I might need to accept?

How have I handled my losses in life?

What limits have I used in my life to keep God and others away?

What are the roles I have gained and lost in my life?

II

Learning to Dance

For some, what could be considered entering a brave, new world is moving one's body in reckless abandon to the beat of music, whether it is waltz music, fifties swing tunes, rock and roll, or hip hop. I grew up loving to dance. My father was an accomplished jitterbug dancer. He competed in contests and was on a televised program with Dick Clark predating *American Bandstand*. I remember attending weddings of family friends and watching my parents cut the rug on the dance floor. I was always pleased when it was my turn to be twirled about, get dizzy, and fly around the floor. One of my favorite pictures from when I was little is a photo of my father waltzing with me at age five, with my feet standing on his large shoes. My face is rather serious as I was, no doubt, trying to learn this new art form. Perhaps for me, a passion for dancing is part of my genetic inheritance.

Swing 101

My husband and I undertook a challenge that I now recommend as a refreshing dose of marriage therapy; we took swing dance lessons. In high school and college, my favorite T-shirt was white with loud, blue print, "TO DANCE IS TO LIVE." With all the peer pressure and existential angst of the teen years, dancing was a release valve for the pressure in my life. I found the music and movement intoxicating, freeing, and delightful. I could easily dance until 4 A.M. and not realize time had passed. I did not do it to meet men or draw attention to myself; I needed it as a space to merely be. My form of dance therapy resonates with lyrics from a popular song. David Wilcox, a folk musician, described it this way in "She's Just Dancing":

> She's just dancing,
> Dancing to the band
>
> But when the sweet-talking hunter sees her move
> His rifle only sees a prize he can capture
> And maybe take her home tonight
> Now watch him circle back around as if he can't quite
>   read
> What the writing on her T-shirt says
> She spells it out and says
> I'm just dancing, OK? OK
>
> Don't try to track her trail hunter
> She is not your game
> This is a wild-life sanctuary
> And wild is why she came[1]

Given my love of dancing and my husband's past inhibitions about this form of movement, I naturally assumed my role as instructor and leader at our first class. This balance of power was quickly disrupted. The true instructor made it very clear that swing does not work that way: I needed to allow my husband space to lead. He assumed his role beautifully, with strength and tenderness (despite a few toe-slams). I had to realize that being in control was detrimental to being able to move as one, flowing through the motions. We had to listen to each other's bodies for clues to the next step. Kirk would move my arm, push against my hand, and pull me in with different pressure to guide me in the swing steps. Along with much laughter, concentration, and a desire not to look foolish, we had a good time.

Another gift from swing lessons were the words, "Don't work on changing your partner; the only person you can change is yourself." Those words have application on and off the dance floor. I was surprised by how simple but true these words are and how difficult they are to execute. It took time for me to turn off my overly sensitive error radar and enjoy our movements, the music, the delight of having a move work out, and the humor of the messes in which we found ourselves. My husband took to these lessons, insisting on practicing before dinner, often spinning me and whatever was on the spatula I was carrying around the kitchen. He purchased tapes so we could watch the pros at home and keep up on our learning. It was a delight, after eight years of marriage, to have my husband fall in love with something I had enjoyed all my life and to be able to partake of it together.

Dancing teaches another lesson: We need to be willing to make mistakes. When I introduce the syllabus every term to a different group of counselors-in-training, I explain that being a learner means risking failure. During the course of the term, they all must face their fear of failure as they "perform" before their peers and their professors. It is critical they all agree to be willing to fail, because that is the precise place they have something to learn. I tell them, "If you do everything right, we have nothing to offer you. You won't be able to see what can be improved. In essence, you do not need to take this class."

Most students look back at me, unconvinced, hoping they will be the first to complete a practicum with a flawless record. However, once the group gets underway, they begin to see that my invitation to them to welcome failure might have some merit. When they recognize what they missed, what went well (that they were unaware of or did not intend—an interesting form of failure), what they said that moved them away from their client and the important matters of the client's heart—they learn. They observe each other's learning experiences and gain wisdom from watching and offering insights.

I can offer words about the need to fail with conviction because I know my failings when I have had to ask forgiveness; I recognize that those are the times that bless others, not my "brilliant" stratagems, analyses, and counselor insights. Failure guards my humility and reminds me I am not in charge of others' repentance, transformation, and sanctification. God is. I can relax because I'm a participant in the process, not the director. Failure is a strange gift that prepares and deepens us for the even greater demands that life will place on us. "From everyone who has been given much, much will be demanded; and from the one who has been entrusted with much, much more will be asked" (Luke 12:48).

A Dance of Words

As a group leader, I find myself surrounded by people who are both excited to grow and deeply resistant to what change will cost them. Leading a group requires agility, as well as intense awareness of what is happening not only for each person present but also within the leader him/herself. When I have forgotten the latter, I have not been successful.

During one of the weeks I was taking fertility medication, I was frustrated at my overcrowded schedule. One of the men in my group started sharing, and I felt irritated. His anger and bullying were effective defenses to ensure that no one would deal with him or offer him any unwanted advice. He was holding everyone in the group at bay and offering little of the substance of what he had presented in previous weeks. He was stubborn about not wanting anything from any of us. However, his speech was smooth and carefully laced with invitation, and the group did their best to address him. As they admitted later, "We did not want to take him on and were glad someone else did." That someone else was me.

After the group exhausted their questions and he sat back with his arms crossed, looking smug and slightly bored, I decided it was time to bring on the hard questioning. I verbally chased after him and took his off-putting remarks in stride. As you might expect, my aggressive approach elicited an equally aggressive response from him, and the group watched as I battled with this man for a half hour. It was not a good fight. Instead of inviting him to dance, I jumped in the boxing ring and was all too willing to put up my fists and fight. In a way, I gave him just what he wanted, which was a tangle he would not let me win. I compromised the goodness of what I had to offer by signing on for this level of struggle. I did not listen to see if my own heart might have cautioned me from proceeding; it was easier to react to him rather than to consider what might be best for him, the group, and myself at that moment. It was one of many failures that I have tasted as a counselor.

After the event, as most counselors might, I questioned whether I should be in the profession. Why had I reacted so strongly to this man? Why had I fallen into his trap and gone down swinging? As a woman, why had I agreed to fight like a man? I was capable of more clever and inviting methods of engagement. Since I had not listened to my heart while leading the group, I knew I had to face its questions to me in the days that followed. It was a humbling week to realize that I should return to the group and highlight that there were better ways to handle the situation. However, as I did so, the outcome surprised me. The group warmed up to me, as did my adversary from the week before; they were more willing to speak of their own failures in that moment and why they had not loved this man better. Our group dance of words and relationships resumed stronger than before. The goodness of those follow-up meetings did not erase my blunder. However, I began to see that my mistakes are opportunities for my growth, and that of others as well. May the dance continue.

What Might It Mean to Dance with God?

While the thought of husbands and wives dancing together may not seem so strange, the thought of dancing with God may not be quite as familiar. As I have wrestled with putting my dancing and faith in perspective, different words have found their way to a page.

Coming Alive

I want to pull my chair up to the Banquet feast. I want to taste, feel, hold, listen to, speak with, and see that the Lord is good. I believe that you are good, Lord.

I want to see colors rightly, the butterfly across the page, the passion of your world, the power of song, of mov-

ing in dance to music, of living a little crazy, on the
wild side, with pure, unadulterated abandon.

I want to be a swan of beauty who finally knows that she
can fly.
Fly soul! Fly spirit! Breathe through me new wind that
once was still and dead.
Race through my trembling limbs to burst forth in
light of multicolored marvel.
Sing through my faltering voice, may it rise loud and
true for you through these small lips and closed eyes.
Dance in me and for me. Bring others into my dance
done to honor you. Sound out the melodic beat, clang
the shrill cymbals. Herald this is the day.
This is the good day
of coming home
of feeling as if for the first time.
Free my thirst to drink deeply of you, my warrior and
king.
Your love awaits for the start of a new dance.

A theme woven throughout Scripture is that of God's
passionate, unfailing pursuit of his people. He makes it
clear his grace is irresistible, and we are called his sons or
daughters. Is this a God who calls us to dance? As I envi-
sion the wedding feast prepared for us in heaven (Revelation has much to say about the event and setting), I imagine there will be dancing. Most weddings involve dancing
as an expression of joy, celebration, and unity. There are
many elements being knit together: husband to wife, wife's
family to husband's, and the community to the blessing of
this new couple. Dancing expresses the fact that our limbs
cannot sit still as we partake of a good event. Movement
is an aspect of participation. God wants all of us, not just
our minds and souls but our bodies and physical expression as well.

From Dying to Dancing

They had spent years dismissing each other: Carl would turn his back on Rita, and she would rage at him. The pattern had been so well worn that neither could remember a time before these seeds of discontent had been sown.

It had started small. He had applied selective hearing to most of what she had asked of him. Her demands seemed so complicated, confusing, and draining to him: "How can I get to all the projects she has for me, her aspirations for my greatness, what she wants, and her emotions?" For her, he quickly fell off the pedestal of being the knight in shining armor she had dreamt of as a little girl: "He has horrible follow-through. I asked him to provide a more secure home for the kids and me. Did he do it? No. He had more important things to do. We always wanted a family vacation. How I would ride him to get promotions, stay home in the evenings, spend more time with his children. Did he listen? No. I am tired of having another kid around the house to manage. This has not been a marriage of two adults. I want out."

A wise counselor at this point would check his or her growing sense of discomfort, dis-ease, and frankly, panic, and remember the words, "I did not get the marriage in this state and I certainly cannot get it out of it."

As I sat across from Carl and Rita, I remembered the words of a seasoned marriage therapist, who told me, "Most people come to marriage counseling three to five years too late." Was it too late for them? I wondered whether they could learn to dance again.

The first order of business was to inform them their marriage was in worse shape than they were letting themselves believe. I pointed out that they had invited me to be the mortician who declared their marriage "no longer viable." But that was not my role—it was theirs. If they wanted to work on restoring the marriage, I would join them. If not,

I advised them not to waste their time or money, or mine. Drastic diagnoses call for strong words, so I reached for my emergency tools. I asked Carl and Rita if they were serious about getting into the messiness of their own sins and failures to see if there were signs of revivable life to this marriage. After a few solemn moments, they assured me they were.

One of the first areas we had to uncover in the weeks ahead was the way that each of them had contributed to the mountain of distrust between them. How had each avoided the call to love one another? How had each abandoned the marital vows repeatedly? That is not only difficult to look at individually but even more so in front of an offending spouse. Carl and Rita decided they wanted to meet individually with me and also together for marital work. Those meetings together allowed for confession times for harm done and received.

Carl had to consider why it was so easy for him to disengage, retreat, and withdraw from relationship. He realized he had a pattern of always finding the easy way out of everything, including dealing with the anger of his childhood home and his own emotions. Carl had become a very hidden, lonely man.

Rita began to face the futility of demanding that her husband change. She became aware of the healing power of telling the truth about her hurt, disappointment, and grief without demanding change of Carl, rather inviting him to know his impact on her and the children.

Both had mastered the art of thwarting the good in the other. They now began learning the language of being present to their spouse and themselves. Over time, when Carl was irritated he was able to put words to how he was feeling without accusing Rita of wrongdoing and without hiding in his shell. Rita was able to see how she fought Carl to avoid facing her own loneliness and sense of emptiness. Rita also became adept at speaking of her heart and desires in ways that invited Carl to move toward her. Rita began celebrating her strength in relationship and found her social life improving.

As we neared the end of our work together, I made the comment that perhaps they might want to consider taking dancing lessons together. They laughed and said, "Didn't we tell you? Tonight is our third waltz class."

Biblical Witness

Miriam's Song (Exodus 15:20–21)

Miriam, the prophetess, was not only a woman of words but also of song and dance. After the dramatic parting of the waters and the vanquishing of their assailants, the Hebrew people stood on the far side of the Red Sea. They had crossed the divide on dry land while Pharaoh and his men suffered a watery fate. Afterward, Moses led a song, as did his sister, Miriam.

She took up a tambourine, with all the women joining her with tambourines and dancing. She sang, "Sing to the Lord, for he is highly exalted. The horse and its rider he has hurled into the sea" (Exod. 15:21).

We can imagine that their beautiful voices lifted high above the returning waves, carrying a sweetness only found in voices recently freed from slavery and inviting all present to tap their feet, clap their hands, and join in the worshipful dance. Celebration time had begun. It was a welcome response to the hectic days of leaving Egypt, being pursued, and then being the objects of God's mercy in his miraculous act of parting water for his people to pass toward the Promised Land. It was a timely celebration, because the days ahead would bring many trials, times of doubt, seeking other gods, hunger, grumbling, waiting, and wandering. On that journey, the desert would feel like a wasteland, making the Israelites long for the days of enslavement when at least they had food. Miriam's song, movement, and sound were a reprieve from the trials of being God's people in the desert. It provided a context to rejoice in, and later to remember God's miraculous provision for his people. This was an important scene to recall when the going got tough.

Do we celebrate God's deliverance, the work of his redemption, his care and concern for our well-being? Do we see worship, whether or not it involves using tambourines, singing songs, and tapping our feet, as acts of thanks to God? Just as back in the days of the exodus, Miriam leads the way.

Study Questions

What do I like and dislike about dancing?

How do I handle my failures?

What might it mean for me to dance with God?

What relationships in my life need some dancing?

How do I celebrate the good things God has done in my life? What holds me back?

12

What We Give Is Good

With all the advances and changing definitions of what it means to be a woman in our North American culture in a new millennium, women are still telling me they sense something is missing.

What does it mean to live a healthy, balanced life in a world that can seem out of control? In our busy lives of juggling multiple demands, roles, and relationships, there seems to be less space for enjoyment. Enjoyment includes things like being able to receive the moments shared with friends and loved ones, a warm mug on a cold morning, and time alone with God. We are too harried to recognize the moments to be enjoyed both outside of ourselves and within. We forget how to enjoy who we are becoming and where God has placed us.

My experience has taught me that women often do not trust or value that which they have to bring to God, themselves, and others. As a way of determining which areas in your life are difficult for you to enjoy, consider your story in light of these two questions: "Which areas of your life have you tried to silence? Which scenes lack color?"

The Gift of Goodness

In chapter five we looked at the gift of sight and what we refuse to see. There we dealt with the harm that we refuse to see, but we also refuse to see our glory. This is often a difficult area for women. Glory comes from two places: the potential God has placed in us and our status as having been adopted into his royal family. We are daughters of a king, but all too often we live as if we are street orphans. We won't own our God-given goodness.

Have you noticed how difficult it is for most women to receive compliments? Someone says, "I like your outfit," and we respond, "Oh, this old thing. It is a little too tight, don't you think?" Or, "Your speech was excellent" gets the reply, "I just threw it together last night." In each case, the responder neglects the simple words that signal having received something: "Thank you." There is something excruciating about acknowledging the goodness God has put in us and letting that stand. It seems even worse to be caught owning goodness in front of others—"They might think I am conceited or boastful." We misuse Christian humility when we use it to justify deprecating God's gift of life, beauty, talents, and strength.

We seem to be afraid to acknowledge the glory and dignity that God has imparted to us. If we were to receive that which God has given and call it "much," we know that more is required of us. God might ask more of us if there really is something good in us to be offered to others. If we recognize the extent of our blessings, the fullness of our cup, maybe we could be offering greater gifts of love and service to others and enjoying God's delight in us as well. That feels risky.

Words of Life in the Face of Death

Part of the process of becoming a licensed counselor includes a minimum of two years of counseling under a seasoned counselor's supervision. My supervisor was a gift, not only to my work with clients but also to my own life. Six years ago, my husband and I had wrestled with infertility for a year. We were overjoyed to discover a month before the first appointment with infertility specialists that we were expecting. I had the opportunity to work through the common "pregnant woman's fear of miscarrying" with my supervisor. I wrestled with God about letting me keep the baby to term. I felt I would lose my mind if anything happened to this child. I was aware I was trying desperately to bargain with God, yet there were no guarantees.

In one particular session, I reported the details of those days of surprise and questions: "After asking the nurse to repeat three times that she did in fact say positive and that positive does in fact mean pregnant, something inside me snapped. It had been a year of tests, hormone supplements, blood drawn, and finally a decision to have a full makeup at a fertility clinic. My husband and I were beginning to accept the reality that only drugs and technology would make us parents. I felt sorrow that only a generation ago I might have been a barren Sarah.

"How did this strange miracle happen? Our appointment at the fertility clinic had been eight weeks away. We had given up trying by human means of control and prediction, fertility drugs, ovulation kits. . . . A resounding chorus of responses to my news was, 'See, when you don't focus on it, it happens.' Having too many beloved friends struggle with infertility, I could not believe that was so. I preferred to view it as our private miracle.

"Because this had come as a long-awaited answer to prayer and yet was still a profound surprise, I worried the first few days. Hearing negative for twelve months and then one day hearing positive requires a radical paradigm shift. My concerns included: They read the wrong test, I haven't been drinking enough water, I've used prescription medications, and had a few glasses of wine. Will I be allowed to keep this child? Somehow the question of deserving this was prominent. I felt I didn't deserve this long-awaited child. My questions of faith became all the more profound. Is God really good? Does he grant us our heart's true desires? Is this life his to give and take as he wills? How can I trust in such ambiguity?

"As the days progressed, this baby seemed tied more to earth through my womb than to a dream in heaven. I felt more hope and trust that this child might in fact be here to stay. Somehow God might even want that for us."

A month later, my supervisor and I were having a very different conversation. Kirk and I felt all the joys, fears, and anticipation of parents-to-be. I was still dealing with morning sickness. It was time for our ten-week checkup. We had seen our child's heartbeat and its small, developing body two weeks earlier. After ten agonizing minutes, the doctor informed us he could not find the baby; it was not there, or at least not in the manner in which it should have been. The doctor told us he feared the baby was not alive.

My husband and I spent the next week in a hellish twilight, walking on the earth but hardly feeling it beneath us. We were not even sure we wanted to. Hope seemed ugly, ludicrous, and mean. God seemed arbitrary, capricious, and cruel. We awaited news and received conflicting responses for the next week. During that time, I continued to teach counseling and theology (about God's goodness and faithfulness) at a graduate school, supervise others, and see clients for my practice. I recall screaming internally at God, "Why are you asking me to give life to others, when quite literally I carry death inside me?" I was a tomb but was still called to offer life. In the heart of my pain, sorrow, and anger at God for seeming to taunt me with getting pregnant, almost making it to my second trimester, I was in the lowest place of low.

During the week we were waiting for test results, my doctor was convinced the pregnancy had terminated, but my hormones kept rising. I knew that this could be a common reaction by the placenta as it tries to make a final, valiant attempt to restore life to what has already been lost. None of the medical professionals had hope for us. Ours was waning as well.

It was into this mess of confusion and angst that my supervisor graciously inserted himself. He asked me an incredibly challenging question: "Is your womb good?" I looked at him, stunned. I thought, *How can he say such a thing? Of course it is not.* At that moment, it was a tomb for a dead, disintegrating child that I would never hold or feel her breath on my cheek. What was this crazy counselor thinking? I politely tried to ignore the question. Undaunted, he offered it again. He said it five or six times in the session—at least that is my memory of what it took until I received it. When I finally acknowledged the question and even began affirming that my womb was good, a wave of relief and peace passed over me. It did not remove the heartache or the questions I had for God, but it did offer me a place to see that all of this from God was not wrong, evil, or destructive. It also removed the weapons of self-contempt that I was all too ready to wield against myself for "losing" my child.

In the five years since that counseling hour, our infertility has persisted. We have remained childless. I still have questions for God that may remain unresolved for a lifetime. Yet I have never doubted the truth given to me that day: "My womb is good." Whether I bear children or not, it is a symbol of my ability to give life to others, to nurture and nourish relationships and help people in their process of becoming. I have come to peace with that part of me and know, in light of my sufferings, that God will use it for good and his glory. He has made me a life giver. This new call found me and has haunted me to glory.

Two Paths

When we are experiencing loss, sadness, and brokenness, there are two ways we can respond. These two paths lead to very different places. We can feel hurt, depleted, and despairing. Or we can face our grief, weeping and trusting God. One road seems to short-circuit and deny our pain while the other takes us right through the heart of our struggle to a new place.

The Path of Diminishing Returns

Jane was adept at quieting her needs in order to attend to everyone else in her life. As a grandmother, community leader, and service coordinator at her church, she could accomplish more than three people running a race. "How does she do it?" her friends and neighbors wondered, admiring her seemingly endless reserves. But what Jane did not admit to herself, or them, was that she was not running *to* something but *from* something. Her son had been killed in an auto accident sixteen years previously, and it was determined that he was on narcotics at the time. As the impact of the event sank in, Jane felt so guilt-ridden and grieved that she made a conscious decision to not feel the emotions that were surfacing: "I will get busy, I will take better care of people than I did my son, I will protect other people's children. . . . " She chose the path of diminishing returns, which demanded that her flight accelerate to keep feelings and memories at bay.

We choose the path of fragmentation when we ignore life's difficulties and try to get around them, rather than through them. As most health care workers will attest, suppressing or refusing to own all our emotions, like unacknowledged anger, can have inward and outward repercussions. We compartmentalize our lives so that each area—work, home, family, social life—is separate from the others, and we live without a sense of integration. Physically, our bodies bear the stress of containing our suppressed feelings. These manifest themselves in ulcers, headaches, high blood pressure, and sleeplessness. Emotionally, we distance ourselves from our heart realities in order to function. Spiritually, we learn to distrust what we see in the world around us. Our relationships with God and others are weakened. Our sense of voice and vision end up diminished.

The Lesser-Traveled Road

Three months into her husband's battle with cancer, Carrie walked away from her law practice. Both young urban professionals, they had seemed to have their life before them. Both were climbing the corporate ladder and believed that all their advanced schooling was finally paying off—school debt would soon be a thing of the past. Until the day test results came back and the prognosis was given: Todd had seven months to live. Todd and Carrie decided the operative words in that sentence were "to live." Prayer became their daily bread, sustaining them in the face of death and defeat. They had seven months of laughing and crying together. They traveled to the extent that Todd was

153

comfortable. They read books aloud to one another. They held hands and tenderly made love. Todd dictated notes of love and thanks to important people in his life. They made plans for his funeral. He put words to his dreams for her future without him. Carrie had determined that she could not go back to law after his death. They dreamt of what she was good at and created a vision for her.

Carrie looked at me with tears in her eyes and said, "I graduate this weekend. How I wish Todd could be here to see that all those dreams we discussed are coming true. I have a job at a Christian clinic to counsel others dealing with grief. I know what it is like to walk through the valley of the shadow of death. I also know there is another side." Todd and Carrie gave each other a tremendous gift: the freedom to live and die with dignity and then to choose to live again.

When we are healing women who believe that what we have to offer is good, we can choose life in the face of death as well. Instead of fragmenting our lives, we can seek to integrate the joys and sorrows of life. We can invite God into our place of struggle and be willing to walk through the valley with him. Our hope comes as we move through an honest self-examination toward life. Even the pathway of grief can be a place for meeting God. In times of loneliness, we encounter the face of a God who grieves with us and who has journeyed on the Way of Sorrows. Grief opens our hearts to new life and freedom. We are free to stop pretending, to take down the mask, and to risk opening our heart to God and others again. Beyond grief, there is the possibility of genuine, rich encounters with others. This can mean deeper friendships and hope for healing. When faced with the option of facing our grief and being free to weep for our pain, which can lead to trusting God and finding rest, will we choose it?

Biblical Witness

God sees our affliction and knows our struggle. Will we admit that our ability to bear life is good?

Hagar (Genesis 16)

I, Hagar, had the unfortunate fate of being in the wrong place at the right time. I was an outsider who became an outcast. How strange that God chose to address me in the beginning of his great story. I was an Egyptian maidservant to Abram and Sarai. It was Sarai's crafty thinking that created the mess out of which my story gets told.

Their God had promised an offspring. When that did not materialize, Sarai gave me to Abram to bear children for her. Although this practice was a common custom, I hated my mistress for this. My child was to be theirs, just as I was not my own person but their slave. My attitude caused strife between Sarai and Abram. He abandoned me to her whim, and she exacted her revenge on me for my fertility and angry heart toward her. After she took a rod to me, I left. I figured I would be better off on my own in the desert than submitting to a beating under their tents.

A strange thing happened to me out there. It took place by a spring, a life-giving place in the otherwise arid desert. I was traveling down a road, east of my homeland, and had stopped for water to assuage my intense thirst. I thought I was safe and alone, but then, suddenly, a figure I had never seen before appeared. He spoke as if he had been looking for me, "Hagar, servant of Sarai, where have you come from, and where are you going?" (Gen. 16:8). I confessed my getaway plan. The angel directed me to go back to Sarai and to abundant descendants of my own. I was told the name of my son.

155

Then I spoke to this mysterious God who had spoken to me. I offered him the substance of who I was, this God I did not even know. I am honored he chose to come after me and reclaim me. I called him "the God who sees me," for "I have now seen the One who sees me" (Gen. 16:13). As a matter of fact, the well where this took place is still called Beer Lahai Roi, which means the well of the Living One who sees me.

Study Questions

Do I doubt that what I give to others is good?

In what areas do I struggle, believing I have nothing to offer to others?

What do I have in me with which to nourish others?

Do I run from my life, or do I face my struggles with integrity?

13

Deepened Friendships

One of the hurdles to deepening our friendships is the fear of being rejected. Our fears keep us isolated and rob us of the joy of knowing others and being known ourselves. We fear someone will disregard our words or dislike us. Sometimes we find excuses for others not to like us and close the door to possible friendships. One of the issues we use to dismiss ourselves is that of age. We may become convinced that we are either too old or too young to offer anything of substance to another person.

Scripture tells us to relax on these accounts. Paul's words to Timothy, "Don't despise your youth," remind us of the importance of giving, even when you are ministering to your elders. Our Christian tradition teaches that age should elicit respect; we are to look at our elders as the ones who speak wisdom. Who better to go to with matters of life and struggles of the soul? Our culture may not respect aging, but biblical testimony certainly does. No matter what your age, loving people and being in healing relationships requires that you be yourself. It is who you are and who your clients are willing to let you be in those moments that count.

God Uses Us Despite Ourselves

Not long into my counseling practice, an older woman appeared at my office to see me for counseling. This woman was old enough to be my mother's mother. As we started meeting, I was aware I felt tense, awkward, and almost apologetic about my words. As I tuned in to my internal barometer, I became aware of my fear concerning our age difference. I wondered, *What could I possibly have to say to this woman with so much life experience?* She had lived a full life and was a well-respected professional who had a significant impact on others. I felt ashamed. Somehow, I made it through the first session. I recall praying afterwards, "Lord, if it is your will, please do not let this woman return, because I believe I have nothing to say to her." I was worried that our session was a terrible waste of time for her.

Despite my prayer, she showed up for our second session. The first thing she said to me was, "I was angry at you when I left last week, and I realized that you reminded me of my mother." Inside, I was jumping up and down with excitement. My sails had been unfurled. Now we were ready to journey somewhere together. She took me seriously and let me matter to her even when I was convinced the opposite should be true. With her words, something in me relaxed—I can speak into this hour and in this relationship. I said a grateful prayer to God.

It never ceases to amaze me how often women have offered me weighty gifts in moments when I am counseling or caring for them. Sometimes I wonder who is really ministering to whom in the moment. Given that a counseling hour is focused on the client, counselors' stories of healing and gifting often go unsaid.

When counseling relationships draw to a close, I often let clients know how encouraging their story, courage, and presence have been to me. In their struggle, pain, defeat, hope, dreams, and love interests, I have had the honor of being a compassionate companion on the journey through their thorny memories and stories of their hearts. Some women have confounded me; others have invited me to a place of worship.

In a mutual friendship, sharing how another has impacted you for good is the fertile soil for future growth. Among friends, stories of inspiration can be shared and acknowledged, which in and of itself offers hope and life.

Comparison—An Impediment to Friendship

A healing woman pays attention to the issues that can exist beneath the surface of her relationships with other women. One issue that needs to be examined is that of competition. Our society feeds women's fears and insecurities by setting us up in comparative relationships with one another: "How do I compare to fashion models or the 'in' styles?" For a consumer society, the manufactured "need" to look a certain way ensures a long line at the beauty counter or even plastic surgeon's office. Comparing women to what they are "supposed to be" can be demeaning; moreover, it sets women against one another.

The dynamic of jealousy and comparison is not new to our experience as women. If we look to Scripture, we find similar struggles between Hannah and Penninah, and

Sarai and Hagar. Even Mary and Martha had a hard time when one slaved away in the kitchen and the other enjoyed the company of Jesus. For Hannah and Sarai, their jealousy was over the topic of fertility. We do not often hear stories about men who are jealous of other men who have a flock of sons. There may be some biblical precedence for women comparing themselves to one another. This category raises a question, "How have I not loved well and offered less than my best to my friend?" Where has that standard of comparison held you back from your friends?

Reading Faces

You may have had the experience of searching for a loved one on a crowded train platform, at a busy amusement park, on a school playground, or on a bustling city street. If you have, you know what it feels like to struggle to discern if that tall man about the height of your brother is, in fact, him. What does it require to be sure? If you know the clothes he is wearing, you have a good chance of finding him, even if he has his back to you. But what if he works in the financial district, and you are in a sea of men with blue suits? The only true test is to see his face. Movies demonstrate this as well, when the cameras pan around a figure until we see his face and finally know the identity of a mysterious character.

What is it about our faces that allows us to be known? There are powerful stories about people living with disfigured faces and how they cope with being different, with people not seeing them for who they are because their faces keep others at a fearful distance. Films such as *The Elephant Man* and *The Man without a Face* visually describe this. Both show the agony of being "unlovely" by cultural standards and therefore feeling rejected and dismissed, even feared and hated. The face is significant.

Faces not only carry with them the marks of our age but also tell a story through our expressions. When a spouse or boyfriend looks at us a certain way, we know whether he is frustrated or delighted in us. When a friend smiles at us, it can communicate celebration, sorrowful understanding, or recognition. We can distinguish each of the smiles, and each communicates something different. Many emotions and thoughts are worn on our faces. Even layers of makeup do not distract us from reading a face. We can see a face on deeper levels. Reading a face is about reading the soul inside that uses expressions, gestures, and a twinkle in the eye to communicate itself. This is a language that takes place even in the absence of words. Our faces speak of our souls.

One of the tremendous gifts that women can offer to one another is to be an honest mirror, a mirror to help us see our faces reflected through the eyes of others. This is especially effective if one woman trusts that the other has her good in mind. It can be a transforming gift to have someone reflect back to you your glory, the realities of your face. But for a mirror to be redemptive, it must be honest. It should reflect not only goodness but sin and struggles as well. This reflective ability increases in strength as the relationship between women deepens. Over time, trust allows each to be more open and willing to receive.

Women have the privilege to be an advocate and friend. It is important, then, to avoid an argument that is based on a power struggle: "Here is what is wrong with you and how you need to change." A comment like that will only engender anger and defensiveness and move the participants away from one another. It draws the worst out of one another—everyone gets hurt and no one leaves a winner. Let us learn to confront one another in ways that neither destroy beauty, nor rob the other of their goodness. It is better to collaborate with your friends for a higher good.

Speaking the Truth in Love

We can feel certain dilemmas when we offer words of truth to a friend. Often we think we do not know what to say or even when to say it.

Constructive Conversation

Let's say you have a friend, Sally, whose son is a musician. He is a respectable teenager, not strong academically, searching for a sense of himself as a young man. His mother is not pleased with his choices. She was a scholar and an engineer, so her son baffles her and frustrates her dreams for him. You think: "I have seen how Sally puts down her son whenever we get together, but it isn't my place to say anything about it. I wouldn't feel so bad about it if it weren't for the fact that he is often within earshot." If you were Sally's best friend, why wouldn't you want to help her grow?

There is a fine art to learning the dance of timing, one of the steps of which is raising curiosity. As we know from the stories of the Old Testament prophets, God's people are capable of ignoring words spoken directly to them for their edification. Even Jesus encountered plenty of people who were not ready to receive the good news he offered. If you know that Sally is prone to defensiveness, you might want to pay attention to when would be a good time to speak. Certainly, if she asks for feedback, the door is wide open for conversation. However, in most relationships, feedback is not often something people are brave enough to invite, even from their most trusted companions. It is a risky step to take. More likely you will have to initiate the dance with a gracious invitation.

In order to find a constructive way into a conversation with Sally, you may need to make a comment or ask a question that will heighten her curiosity—a sense of intrigue lowers defenses. For instance, you might want to ask her about her relationship with her son, specifically, how they are working through differences or conflict. You might want to make a statement about how difficult it is for you and your spouse to get along because one of you is an artist and the other a scientist. If she responds with interest, you may want to invite her to consider, "I am sure you wrestle with this all the time with your son. It is hard accepting that those we love are different than we may have hoped or planned, but that doesn't necessarily make them wrong. What do you think?"

Approaching important issues delicately and gradually allows the other person to acquire ears to hear and softens their heart to receive the truth. In response to your gentle movement toward her heart, many an honest Sally might offer a response, "I am aware that at times my heart is not for my son. I have critiqued him in ways that are hurtful and made him pay for not being just like me. I wonder if he and I need to have a chat." Well-timed words can open a heart to truth. They can also allow the person to own their wrongdoing without the friend needing to force truth on her in a shaming way.

Intervention

Remembering Moses' story in Exodus 17, sometimes we need to be friends who hold up others' arms, to support their efforts to do what is right and to make godly choices. You may be asked to hold another's arms in order for God's good to be made manifest in a situation. Are there moments for more powerful and intrusive words than I was recommending above? Yes. There are times friends are living out self-destructive patterns that require more direct intervention. An intervention is a process of con-

163

fronting an addict with their choices and its relational consequences; it can be a real gift to a friend who is substance-addicted. They may not receive it as such in the moment, but with treatment and time, they may return and say, "Thank you for caring enough to stand up to and for me." Also, when you are concerned that a friend is despairing of life, you need to intervene; this can include strongly encouraging them to go to counseling and even calling the police because you suspect that they may be about to take their own life. In extreme moments, tough love is required. That is part of the gift of being healing women; sometimes we must reach out to other women who need healing but are not sure they have sufficient strength to reach for it themselves.

Making Known the Gift of Presence

Along with being a mirror, women can enhance each other's sense of presence. This means helping them recognize their presence, that is, their substance and their impact on others.

A Positive Impact

Many women do not realize that their presence communicates without words. Women often feel like they need to perform or prove themselves to matter or have weight in others' lives. But do you know that when you walk into a room the mood changes and it is different than it was before you arrived? We often do not realize that simply by entering a room we bear presence. Our presence can speak of our soul.

Imagine a person you deeply respect and admire who you have not seen in a long time. What if they were to enter the room right now? What would you feel? My guess is that you would jump up, put down this book, and give them a big hug. You would be wearing an irrepressible smile and want to invite them to sit, talk, or share a cup of tea. Your reaction is an example of how someone's presence can change a scene and your heart in the moment—simply by showing up in your world.

A Negative Impact

Unfortunately, we can also present ourselves in a negative light. Presence can also speak of the walls people have constructed around their hearts to keep others out. "Oh no, here comes Aunt Josie; I wonder who's in trouble now!" The woman who inspires comments like this has set people up to expect disapproval or rejection. She is offering a very different kind of presence to others. However, for someone like Aunt Josie, that is not the full story. Even she would love for people to jump up and run across the room to give her a hug, but her life and struggles have hardened her from hoping for such a gift. Instead, she ensures people will be there for her by maintaining control. Her relationships consist of coerced and obligated care, not freedom in action, on the part of those around her. Don't let appearances fool you: People may want more and hope for good from others when they appear the least in need. They are the squeaky wheel that requires grease but would much rather have love.

For an Aunt Josie, again, well-timed words and raising curiosity may be catalysts for change as she begins to see that she wants love and receives dutiful obedience. Even for her, change is possible. She needs someone strong enough in her life to tell her, "I will not let you intimidate me from standing up to you. I expect better of you than to settle for the demeaning ways you treat others." This can often be done effectively if communicated playfully: "You sound awfully grumpy today. I know that isn't really how you feel about visitors."

It is also important to point out that Aunt Josie's style of interacting is not always successful. For instance, honest love would inform her that there are consequences to her choices: "I suppose the neighbors do not want to come by since you yelled at them last month about their dog. Do you think there are any options for dealing with this situation? What would you like to see happen? What will you choose?" Avoid the trap of offering advice to someone in this condition. It will only fall on deaf ears and may ensnare you further, as they come to think of you as someone who will take on the burden of living for them.

Dream Recoverers

I have always found archeology fascinating. I suppose it is the recovery of stories of people long past that intrigues me. Here were women who wore jewelry, went to the public baths, cooked meals for their families in bowls similar to those I use, and lived two thousand years ago. They had children for whom they hoped and dreamed, spouses that went off to war, and no idea that Mount Vesuvius would change all that in a moment. We live with the same degree of daily details and against the same backdrop of uncertainty. Will I learn from their lesson and live more fully in the now, rather than anticipate my tomorrows?

Archeology bears a close resemblance to the work of healing women. Whether you work with women as friends or clients, you have the opportunity to help restore someone's dreams. What is it they wanted to be or dreamed of becoming when they felt closer to God and the future seemed brighter? Where have they abandoned the hope they knew and chosen to settle for something familiar rather than reach for the impossible that only God might make possible? That is part of the holy calling of friendship. For example, you know your friend desired to be an artist because you have seen pictures of her at seven years old with paintbrush, a beret, and easel, so for her birthday, you sign the two of you up for a drawing class and provide her with the first sketchbook of her adult life. You have studied her well.

I received a very special birthday present from my husband the year we got married. He had heard me mention several times that I always dreamt of flying a plane. When I opened an envelope that indicated I had a flying lesson in a Cessna the next day, I felt incredible excitement and panic. I was stunned. I never expected someone to offer such a gift—or that I would have to put my money where my mouth is and follow through on such a desire.

It was a cold morning as we walked onto the tarmac at Westchester Airport with our instructor. We approached the smallest plane I had ever been in, and my brave spouse decided to climb aboard for the experience. Up we went, ascending in altitude, and my instructor was quick to turn the controls over to me. I was grateful that he had his own set in case I made a major mistake. It frustrated me how relaxed he seemed and how disinterested he was in the controls. I did not know what I was doing. In my fear, I decided it would have been wise of him to be perched, ready to grasp control and redirect the plane. We flew high above my hometown, then on to New York City with a majestic flight down the Hudson. We circled the Statue of Liberty three times and headed back to the airport.

The landing struck terror in me. My trusting instructor kept calmly telling me each next step as he radioed in our arrival to the tower. I kept offering, "I think you should take over now; it only seems right that you should land the plane." He responded, "Don't worry; these planes practically land themselves." I started to perspire. This must be what survival training feels like. Despite my misgivings,

167

the plane did, in fact, glide to a smooth touchdown on the runway, and amazingly enough, mine were the only set of hands on the controls.

I am sure that day and that gift changed me. I lived a dream and faced many fears in the experience. My husband had been a student, even a detective, of my passions. He had listened well to stories of my dreams that I had not even realized I was telling. That is what a good friend, love, child, parent, or counselor can do: Listen to their dreams, remember them, help the other move into them with courage and support. I could not have flown that day without my instructor, but I also may not have had the strength or bravery to stay in control had not the giver of the gift sat behind me, taking pictures and speaking calmly. Living out our dreams can give us back something of ourselves we may have lost or overlooked along the way.

Loving Transformatively

A good friend sees her friend with a heart of compassion, hears her unspoken dreams, prays about speaking the truth in love, and provides a mirror to allow her friend to be seen, warts and all, while still knowing that she is loved.

Healing women help each other discover their beauty, voice, and substance. They bring to light the areas that another may be blind to. Many women do not know how important and decisive of a role they play for others.

For example, a woman may not realize how much her daughter wants her to attend a soccer game or delights in her attention (especially if she is at the age when to show that to Mom is "uncool"). I had the privilege of learning this lesson when I worked with junior and senior high groups at churches. On retreats and in meetings, the young people would confess how much their parents' opinions mattered to them on issues of religion, politics, morality, and themselves. As parents offered tired smiles of appreciation to me on Sunday morning, I realized I knew something they may not have known: Their teenagers really loved and respected them even if they were warring at home.

This same truth applies beyond the scope of parenting teens to other arenas in life. Whether it is a women's group, workplace, volunteer committee, or church, there is often a dearth of honest words of appreciation and thanksgiving. Do we take time to acknowledge not only a task completed but also the manner and artistic elegance with which it was done? How far will we go in offering a compliment? How sad that we reserve the words we really feel about one another for eulogies or a third party. I have often heard women speak glowingly of one another, but I am quite sure those same words were not given directly to their subject. It may feel risky to offer those compliments, but they can be a life-transformative gift in the life of another.

Healing women walk the road of grief with one another. They do not offer the quick solutions or advice of Job's friends; rather they wait, join, and sit with their friend in silence or the honoring gift of a few well-timed words.

Part of the process of deepening intimacy in relationships involves failure: When your friends fail you, speak with them about it instead of discarding them, punishing them, or ignoring the offense. In the process of speaking truth in love, offer a heart that is playful; be kind and offer grace. Finally, enjoy and encounter one another as God lovingly does in his triune nature. Father, Son, and Holy Spirit are eternally in a loving relationship. The image of our Creator provides us with a wonderful example of mutuality and love; we are made in that image, and we are called to grow in it in ever increasing glory.

Biblical Witness

The Weight of His Arms (Exodus 17:1–16)

Moses delivered, interceded for, and led God's people to a place of promise, freedom, and blessing. He was uniquely called but was the first to say, "I stutter; send someone else who can speak for me." He was unwilling to believe God had sufficiently equipped him for the task he laid before him.

By the time we meet him in our passage, Moses had undergone the fears of the Israelites, the pursuing Egyptians, and the parting of the Red Sea. During the crossing, Moses raised his arms, and God held the waters back. Not only Moses' tongue but also his arms of faith were tools for the implementation of God's plan.

Later in Exodus, we are told there is another instance of his arms being symbols of Israel's welfare and good: at Rephidim, when Joshua obeyed God and fought the Amalekites. Moses had told him the day before, "Tomorrow I will stand on top of the hill with the staff of God in my hands" (v. 9). Moses, in obedience to God, stretched out his arms to uphold victory for Israel against the Amalekites. As his arms grew tired, his people began to lose—something had to be done. "When Moses' hands grew tired, they took a stone and put it under him and he sat on it. Aaron and Hur held his hands up—one on one side, one on the other—so that his hands remained steady till sunset" (v. 12).

This presents a powerful picture of love, support, and stepping in on behalf of another for God's will to be achieved. While Joshua fought with the Amalekites, Moses stood and reached to the heavens in intercession. It took more than his personal strength and stamina; it took props and people to keep him strong in the hour of need. His friends—a brother and a builder of the temple—came alongside and offered the needed support. These two believed in the messenger enough to keep him going in the path God had set before him. Hur and Aaron were given the gift of being friends alongside Moses, arm carriers who held the weight of the war and the cause of their people in their supportive hands.

Will you bear the weight of another's arms for the good of God's kingdom? That is what may be required of us as we work for transformation and for God's redemption to be made manifest.

Study Questions

When I think of my friendships, how do I compare myself to others?

Which friends provide me with an honest mirror?

In what relationships might I be able to speak the truth in love?

How do I make a positive and negative impact on others?

How can I help those I love recover their dreams?

Who needs me to help hold up the weight their arms are bearing at this time?

171

14

Being Women of Healing

In Psalm 30 we read: "You turned my wailing into dancing; you removed my sackcloth and clothed me with joy, that my heart may sing to you and not be silent. O Lord my God, I will give you thanks forever" (vv. 11–12). Will we enter into the abundant feast set before us? It will take courage to do so. This Scripture highlights an important aspect of being God's people: Gratitude is central to living out a life of healing. Gratitude does not mean forgetting what has happened or minimizing the struggle. It means moving in and through the pain to get to the other side, the place of dance, joy, and song. Thankfulness knits our hearts to God, strengthens our roots in him, and allows us to keep growing.

Psalm 30 reflects a heart of praise—healing has transpired. In verse 5, the psalmist echoes the end of the Psalm, "weeping may remain for a night, but rejoicing comes in the morning." As we work with our story, soul, and substance, our hearts turn to God first with questions, supplications, anger, and confusion. As we face truth with integrity, we become freed to praise God's unfailing love. Paul writes in Galatians 5:1, "Christ has set us free." We are given freedom and no longer need to be chained to sin. Now that we realize our lives are worth something and that God has placed good within us, we are responsible before him. The root of the word *responsible* reminds us to be responders to God.[1] We are able to give back to him for what he has given us.

Gratitude frees our hearts to deepen our relationship with God. It also invites us to deeper places of connection with others around us. As we receive God's healing, we become healers offering others the cup of compassion.

True Intimacy

If it is true that we become what we dream, we need to consider what keeps us from dreaming. In this book we have looked at some of the resistances and fears and have contrasted them with the benefits and challenges of being faithful women who seek healing and to be healers. In the area of improved relationships, we move from being seekers of healing to being givers of healing. In order to fulfill the task of being better lovers of others, our definitions of love and intimacy may need to be challenged.

In relationships of women to women and women to men, obvious obstacles such as fear of rejection and dismissal, past pain, self-doubt, and isolating anger impede our love. How can we love more fully? We have true intimacy when we enjoy connection with another, which

173

involves desire. Desire includes expectation; we eagerly await a sense of fulfillment, which includes receiving. In this statement, intimacy involves mutual respect and honor. Notice that connection has two movements. First, we put ourselves in the position of desiring. When we desire we are vulnerable, we admit our needs, and we await another's response without demanding or manipulating it. The second movement of intimacy is fulfillment. When someone offers us that cup of compassion, kind word, or understanding nod or compliment, our response is to receive it. Our natural tendency to minimize others' kindness or our need can mute the power of an intimate moment between two people.

Most of us experience false intimacy and think of that as relationship. Many of my clients have age-old frustrations and disappointments with significant people in their lives—parents, spouses, children—but have never put words to what it is they most hope for or dream of regarding that relationship. They are afraid of the price of further disappointment, or even rejection. Desire is too costly. It means that others know of their need and requires that others come through for them. At these times, honesty is avoided, which inhibits the other person from responding freely, so there can be no genuine fulfillment. A nonauthentic relationship does not provide an enjoyable connection; it can leave both parties isolated, angry, or dissatisfied.

Another example of false intimacy is pornography. Those who purchase this material are dealing with misplaced desire; they experience neither fulfillment nor relationship as an end product. There is no connection with another.

We must be present with others to experience connection and enjoyment. We are present with someone when we can "be" with them without the pressure to do anything. When we can walk in their shoes, sit by their side, and offer ourselves, our words are secondary to the power of being with another.

Redemption Is Real

The internal realm is where we struggle and grow, where our core identity resides. As we have journeyed together in this book, my hope has been that you think of the process of change as interesting, involved, and exciting. Perhaps you find yourself drawn to consider the deeper issues underlying how you have chosen to live your life, rather than to focus on changing external behaviors and habits. When we face the darkness of our hearts as well as the redeemed goodness, we can deepen our understanding of volition and thereby find hope. Our ability to choose a different tomorrow, new dreams, and more open ways of relating reflects the power of God's transformative love. We are not bound to continue the mistakes of yesterday or last year. Change is possible.

If I did not believe that to be true, I could not be a counselor. My experience has taught me that redemption is real: My clients and students live it. Their hearts have chosen to live differently. They have walked with God as he brought healing, song, and dance to them. They have collaborated with the movement of the Spirit to courageously face difficult parts of their stories and themselves. These women and men have made themselves vulnerable to change out of a desire to grow, love, and be people of healing.

The Face of a Woman of Healing

What does a woman of healing look like? She is a nurturer who, in turn, is nurtured by a web of relationships, yet she is also distinguishable from them. She has an ability to function well in her daily life. While she is capable, she is also more than the work of her hands. She is able to work hard, but she knows a deep place of rest in the midst of the demands of life. Her self-awareness is evident in her bold laughter at the future. She is willing to face what life brings. She can stand up to the storm because she knows how to admit her need, to be weak as well as strong, to rejoice as well as mourn. She has achieved wisdom that comes from a life of loving and being loved—God's greatest gifts. She believes in the veracity of God's message through Scripture. She hopes for the day her desire will find its fulfillment in God's gracious good.

The woman of healing is aware of her need for God. She sees her sin, yet she is a prodigal daughter because she has experienced the overwhelming gift of grace, new life, and compassion for others. She is willing to fail and bear the price of fear, anxiety, as well as the wounds of others' harm. She knows the weight of being misunderstood, overlooked, ignored, even hated. She responds by weeping for her enemies. In situations of abuse, she refuses to stand in the path of destruction to comply with others' evil. From a distance, she prays and hopes for the day of the abuser's change of heart and glorification. She refuses to belittle or prejudge others, knowing the continuing darkness in her own heart. Her sin awareness allows her to offer grace to others in their darkness. She sees beyond the material to the invisible promise of God's work in others' lives.

She refuses to allow her heart to become hardened. She embraces tears, yet remains open to those who wound. But she still refuses to be battered by others' aggression. She gives what she feels she doesn't have to confirm the truth of the gospel. She allows God's Spirit to supply the needed strength in her present circumstances. She nourishes relationships. She values the closeness of being known and knowing others.

176

The woman of healing is not afraid to face the storms when they come. She can surround herself with loving faces to support her, she can tell her story even when it is difficult, and she can relax in the knowledge that she can do more than pretend with those close to her. She can risk being authentic and honest about her life. She recognizes that as part of a balanced, restored, healing life, there are moments to be with community as well as times to be alone with God.

Biblical Witness

A Warrior Woman (Judges 4–5)

From under a palm tree, she judged and led the people of Israel. A woman prophetess, she spoke for God to a people whose ears had grown dull and hearts cold. She is known as "a mother in Israel" (5:7). Instead of simply passing on God's words of instruction for Barak to accomplish, she was recruited for a dangerous task: In order to bolster his waning courage, she joined Barak in leading the troops into battle. On the battlefield, it was Deborah who sounded the call that drove the men into battle, reminding them that God has "gone ahead of you" (4:14). After victory, she and Barak sang praises to God in celebration of his victory and faithfulness.

It is evident from her story that Deborah played a critical role in her world, both spiritually and politically. She was a powerful change agent who was willing to step into any arena God called her to for the sake of her people and his service. In her love for God and others, she is named the mother of Israel. For the sake of relationships, she was willing to enter battle for good to prevail.

We may be invited to enter other battlefields, such as broken relationships, misunderstandings, poverty, illness, despair, or any area that needs reconciliation. We can be God's courageous warriors for his goodness to triumph.

Deborah models a woman who is willing to speak words of life, command, and purpose. She knows she has something good to offer and believes enough in God's work in her to speak on his behalf. She offers the gift of sight to those blind to God's purposes. Faithfulness is an attribute of beauty. Deborah's conviction in God's provision and leading allow her to be expectant and sure that his purposes will prevail. The enemy's death is at the hands of another woman, Jael. Deborah does not hold back in praising her. In her song we hear the words, "most blessed of women" repeated twice by Deborah and Barak (5:24). Jael is celebrated with even greater words than Deborah. When God's work is done, there is enough room for many to be honored. As a woman warrior, Deborah is more than willing to highlight the achievements of other women and men as they join in the battle (or the dance) of God.

May we live with the same courage, integrity, and passion for the purposes of our great God who rejoices in our transformation and invites us to celebrate our lives with him in a glorious dance. As women who have received healing, may we offer to be healers of other women as well.

Study Questions

What in me has felt healed by God? What areas still await his healing touch?

With whom do I share a relationship of intimacy in which both enjoyment and fulfillment are present?

Do I really believe change is possible?

Since I have tasted healing, what might it mean to offer it to others in my life?

In what battlefields, like Deborah, is God calling me to fight?

How has God's story of redemption for the world through his Son captured my heart and begun a process of change in me? How is the salvation story true in my life?

Notes

Chapter 2 Encountering Men

1. John Gray, *Men Are from Mars, Women Are from Venus* (New York: HarperCollins, 1992).

2. Heather Webb, "Many Come in Darkness: A Conversation with Macrina Wiederkehr," *Mars Hill Review* 9 (fall 1997): 74.

3. Søren Kierkegaard, *Stages on Life's Way* (New York: Schocken, 1967).

4. Simone de Beauvoir, *The Second Sex* (New York: Alfred A. Knopf, 1989), 152.

5. Selecta in Exodus 17.17, quoted in Rebecca M. Groothuis, *Women Caught in the Conflict* (Grand Rapids: Baker, 1994), 195.

Chapter 4 Stories of Difference

1. Anthony Thiselton, *Interpreting God and the Postmodern Self* (Grand Rapids: Eerdmans, 1995), 160.

Chapter 5 The Place of Beauty

1. Quoted by Huston Smith on a Bill Moyers special, *The Wisdom of Faith with Huston Smith,* PBS Production, 1996.

2. Rob Becker, *In Defense of the Caveman,* play (performed in Washington, D.C., 1994).

3. George A. Panichas, ed., *The Simone Weil Reader* (Wakefield, R.I.: Moyer Bell, 1977), 404.

4. Ibid., 405.

5. Ibid., 467.

6. Ibid., 466.

Chapter 6 The Gift of Sight

1. Sue Monk Kidd, *The Dance of the Dissident Daughter* (San Francisco: HarperSanFrancisco, 1996), 15, 18.

2. For more on this topic, see Don Postema, *Catch Your Breath: God's Invitation to Sabbath Rest* (Grand Rapids: CRC Publications, 1997).

Chapter 7 Accepting Our Bodies

1. Maya Angelou, *The Complete Collected Poems of Maya Angelou* (New York: Random House, Inc., 1994), 130–31.

2. Ibid., 130.

Chapter 8 Women Who Inspire Us

1. Dar Williams, *The Honesty Room* (New York: Razor Tie Music LP, 1995), CD.

2. Ibid.

3. Heather Webb, "Grammy Alice," in Traci Mullins, ed., *Grandmother's Touch* (Ann Arbor, Mich.: Servant Publications, 2001), 160–62.

4. Heather Webb, "Favorite Images of the Virgin Mary," *Christianity and the Arts* 8, no. 4 (fall, 2001): 25.

5. David McLellan, *Utopian Pessimist: The Life and Thought of Simone Weil* (New York: Poseidon Press, 1990), 104.

6. Panichas, 15.

7. Ibid.

8. Macrina Wiederkehr, *A Tree Full of Angels: Seeing the Holy in the Ordinary* (San Francisco: HarperSanFrancisco, 1988), 89.

Chapter 9 Expectancy

1. Donald Palmer, *Sartre for Beginners* (New York: Writers and Readers Publishing, 1995), 69–70.

2. Edward M. Cifelli, ed. and comp., *The Collected Poems of John Ciardi* (Fayetteville: University of Arkansas Press, 1997), 254.

3. Wiederkehr, 47.

Chapter 10 The Blessing of Limitation

1. Susan C. Cloninger, *Theories of Personality: Understanding Persons,* 2d ed. (Upper Saddle River, N.J.: Prentice-Hall, 1996), 170.

Chapter 11 Learning to Dance

1. David Wilcox, "She's Just Dancing," *Home Again* (Uni/ A & M, 1991), CD.

Chapter 14 Being Women of Healing

1. Emil Brunner, quoted by Alister E. McGrath, *The Christian Theology Reader* (Cambridge: Blackwell Publishers, 1995), 242–46.

Heather P. Webb teaches in the areas of counseling, theology, and spiritual formation at Mars Hill Graduate School, while maintaining a private counseling practice. She holds an M.Div. from Princeton Theological Seminary, an M.A. in counseling from Colorado Christian University, and a D.Min. from San Francisco Theological Seminary. Heather is also an ordained minister in the Presbyterian Church of the United States of America. She and her husband, Kirk, live in Seattle, Washington.

248.843
W366

113893

LINCOLN CHRISTIAN COLLEGE AND SEMINARY

3 4711 00178 4299